COUNTERING
TRUTH DECAY A RAND Initiative to Restore the Role of Facts and Analysis in Public Life

PROFILES OF NEWS CONSUMPTION

Platform Choices, Perceptions of Reliability, and Partisanship

MICHAEL POLLARD | JENNIFER KAVANAGH

RAND
CORPORATION

For more information on this publication, visit www.rand.org/t/RR4212

Library of Congress Cataloging-in-Publication Data is available for this publication.
ISBN: 978-1-9774-0343-8

Cover: csvbbass9455/stock.adobe.com and BillionPhotos.com/stock.adobe.com
Cover design by Pete Soriano

Support RAND
Make a tax-deductible charitable contribution at
www.rand.org/giving/contribute

www.rand.org

Preface

The information ecosystem is changing rapidly, with new forms of media and news outlets and an array of different types of content. As a result of these changes, the decisions made by news consumers have become increasingly complex and varied. This report examines how people access news, what their assessments are of the reliability of different news media platforms, and how their news consumption profiles or other personal and demographic characteristics shape those consumption decisions and perceptions of reliability.

The report is one of a series funded by internal RAND Corporation funds and published through RAND's Office of the President that focuses on the topic of *Truth Decay*, defined as the diminishing role that facts and data play in today's political and civil discourse. The original report, *Truth Decay: An Initial Exploration of the Diminishing Role of Facts and Analysis in American Public Life* by Jennifer Kavanagh and Michael D. Rich, was published in January 2018 and laid out a research agenda for studying and developing solutions to the Truth Decay challenge. This report is part of that initiative.

RAND Ventures

The RAND Corporation is a research organization that develops solutions to public policy challenges to help make communities throughout the world safer and more secure, healthier and more prosperous. RAND is nonprofit, nonpartisan, and committed to the public interest.

RAND Ventures is a vehicle for investing in policy solutions. Philanthropic contributions support our ability to take the long view, tackle tough and often-controversial topics, and share our findings in innovative and compelling ways. RAND's research findings and recommendations are based on data and evidence, and therefore do not necessarily reflect the policy preferences or interests of its clients, donors, or supporters.

Funding for this venture was provided by gifts from RAND supporters and income from operations. For more information about RAND Ventures, visit www.rand.org/giving/ventures.

Contents

Figures and Tables

Figures

Tables

Summary

In this report, we explore how U.S. media consumers obtain news. We examine the types of dissemination *platforms* (different forms of media delivery; e.g., online, television, print) that consumers rely on and the relationship between consumers' *news consumption profiles* (the specific mix of news platforms consumed; e.g., print and broadcast television, radio, social media) and their overall perceptions of media reliability and the reliability of specific news platforms. We also explore the extent to which people use platforms that they have identified as reliable and their willingness to seek out news from viewpoints that are different from their own, in light of interest in and concern about echo chambers or filter bubbles. Finally, we consider the extent to which demographic characteristics and political partisanship are linked to each of these aspects of news consumption.[1] Using a nationally representative survey of English-speaking individuals 21 and older, we address several questions:

- How do Americans get their news?
- How are news consumption choices linked to demographic or political characteristics?
- Do news consumers believe the reliability of news has changed, and which news platforms do they believe to be more or less reliable?
- How is the perceived reliability of news associated with news consumption choices?

---

[1] Here and elsewhere in this report, we define *partisanship* as an individual's tendency to support one particular group, cause, or viewpoint over another. We measure this through self-rated political ideology and voting behaviors.

In pursuing these questions, we aim to advance the discussion about the relationships among media consumption, trust in media, and *Truth Decay*—the diminishing reliance on facts, data, and analysis in American public life.

Key Findings

News Consumption Profiles

The analysis identified four news consumption profiles differentiated by clusters of how frequently individuals relied on different combinations of several news platforms:[2] print and broadcast television platforms, online platforms (e.g., newspaper websites, such as nyt.com), radio, and social media (e.g., Twitter and Facebook) and in-person communication. Print and broadcast television were commonly used together, as were social media and in-person communication. Note that although we measured cable television use, these data did not help differentiate profiles of news consumption because cable television use was ubiquitous as an important news platform for a large portion of individuals. An individual's news consumption patterns are reflected in how highly they score on all four of these profiles.

Identifying these news consumption profiles and their links to other aspects of news consumption represents a key contribution of this report. These profiles are useful for several reasons. Most importantly, they provide a more holistic picture of news consumers, allowing us to identify which types of sources are often used together and the specific demographic characteristics associated with specific patterns of news consumption. These consumption profiles can be fur-

---

[2] News consumption profiles were determined from a survey conducted in February and March 2018 of 2,543 English-speaking members of the RAND American Life Panel (ALP), which consists of 6,000 U.S. respondents ages 18 and older who regularly take surveys over the internet. The survey asked a randomly selected subset of the panel about their perceptions of the reliability of various sources of news and about how they most frequently got their national and international news. We used factor analysis to identify common patterns in information access within the sample. Respondents reported their relative level of use of print, broadcast television, cable television, online news platforms, radio, social media, and in-person communication to access the news. This approach was data-driven in that the groupings were determined from patterns and combinations in the data rather than being predefined.

ther linked to perceptions about news and news consumption behaviors above and beyond demographic influences.

In comparing the news consumption profiles, we determined that each profile has a distinct set of demographic characteristics. Among them are the following:

- People whose primary news sources are *social media and in-person contacts* are generally younger and female, and they tend to have less education than a college degree and lower household incomes.
- People whose primary news sources are *print publications and broadcast television* tend to be significantly older, and they are less likely to be married.
- People whose primary news source is *radio* are significantly more likely to be male, less likely to be retired, and more likely to have a college degree.
- People whose primary news sources are *online platforms* are significantly younger, more likely to be male and have a college degree and higher income, and less likely to be black.

Taken together, older individuals reported relying primarily on more-traditional platforms (print/broadcast television) for news; younger people reported relying more heavily on social media and in-person communication or on online platforms. Women were more likely than men to report getting their news through social means (social media or in-person contacts). Non-Hispanic white respondents were generally more likely than others to report relying heavily on the social media/in-person and online platforms for obtaining their news.

In parallel with identifying news consumption profiles, we used the survey data to explore how respondents participated in the Hillary Clinton–Donald Trump presidential election in 2016 and how their news consumption (as measured here) was linked to their involvement in the race (e.g., via social media). Our analysis indicates that partisanship and voting behavior appear to be linked to news consumption behavior. This manifested itself in several ways:

- Voters who backed someone other than Clinton or Trump in 2016 were more likely than those who voted for Clinton to score highly on the social media/in-person profile.

- Respondents who rated their political ideology as more liberal were somewhat more likely to be in the online group than those who rated themselves as more conservative.
- Respondents who reported voting for Trump were significantly less likely to score highly on the print/broadcast and online news consumption profiles than those who voted for Clinton.

Reliability of News Media

We also asked respondents to share their perceptions regarding whether the news media have become more or less reliable than in the past and to rank types of news platforms by perceived reliability.[3]

Overall, our survey respondents had mixed perceptions about the general reliability of the news. Although 44 percent reported that they believed "the news is as reliable now as in the past," nearly the same amount—41 percent—reported a belief that the news has become less reliable, while a minority (15 percent) said that they believed that the news is more reliable now. People who were retired, had higher incomes, or voted for someone other than Clinton were significantly more likely to believe the news is less reliable now. Black or Hispanic individuals, those with less education than a college degree, and those who voted in 2016 (versus nonvoters) all were more likely to report that the news is more reliable now. There was also an association between news consumption profiles and perceptions of reliability: People who relied more heavily on online, radio, and social media/in-person platforms to obtain news were less likely to say that news is more reliable now than in the past. Perceptions of how the reliability of news has changed over time were linked to consumption behaviors; those who said the news is more reliable now were more likely to report that they "always or almost always" seek out differing viewpoints in their news than those who did not perceive a change; those who believed the news

---

[3] We use the term *reliability* instead of *trust* because we are more interested in perceptions of media information than of institutions and because we are more interested in the extent to which respondents view various sources as dependable rather than trustworthy. However, our analyses do establish that reliability and trust are correlated.

is less reliable now than in the past were less likely to rely heavily on news from platforms they themselves rated as most reliable.

Perceptions of Most-Reliable Platforms

Broadcast and cable television were perceived to be the most-reliable platforms by the largest number of people in our survey. The reliability of other platforms was ranked as follows: print, online news sites, radio, social media, and in-person communication. People generally reported getting news from sources they rated as the most reliable—particularly those who relied more heavily on print and broadcast television. The exceptions were people who reported getting most of their news from social media and in person despite those platforms' low reliability rankings and people who believed that the news is less reliable now than in the past.

Search for Alternative Viewpoints

An additional aspect of news consumption behavior that we asked about was "how often do you seek out sources of news that you know will offer views that are different from your own?" This question was motivated by recent attention to the negative effects of echo chambers and *filter bubbles*, defined by Merriam-Webster as "an environment and especially an online environment in which people are exposed only to opinions and information that conform to their existing beliefs."[4] One in five respondents (20 percent) reported that they "always or almost always" seek out different views; most people (54 percent) said that they "sometimes" do; 17 percent said that they "infrequently" seek out differing sources; and 9 percent said they "never or almost never" do.

Married people were particularly less likely to report that they "always or almost always" seek out opposing news sources (versus "sometimes" or "infrequently"); black respondents and those of other races were significantly more likely than others to report "never or almost never" doing so. Respondents with higher education and higher incomes were significantly less likely than others to respond that they "never or almost never" seek out opposing news sources. Furthermore, people who scored highly in the online news consumption profile were significantly

---

4 Merriam-Webster, "Filter Bubble," webpage, undated.

more likely to report "always or almost always" seeking out sources of news that offer differing viewpoints and significantly less likely to report that they "never or almost never" seek out differing views. Individuals who said that they perceived any change (either increase or decrease) in reliability of news now compared with the past were less likely to report "never or almost never" seeking out differing views in the news than those who did not believe there had been a change (although only those who believed the news is more reliable now were more likely than those who did not believe there had been a change in reliability to report "always or almost always" seeking out differing views).

Looking at these results in terms of partisanship and voting behavior patterns also could provide interesting insights. People who rated their general political ideology as more liberal were more likely to report that they "never or almost never" sought out sources that they knew would offer views that are different from their own, as were those who voted for Clinton (compared with those who voted for Trump). Taken together, this suggests that, compared with other voters or non-voters, those who voted for Clinton are less skeptical of more-traditional news delivery platforms, tend to favor print as their source for news, are much less likely to believe that the reliability of news has declined over time, and are less likely to rate online or in-person news as the most-reliable platforms. Those who voted for Clinton were also less likely than other voters to report that they "always or almost always" seek out news sources that offer views different from their own. Furthermore, those who did not vote in the 2016 presidential election were less likely than others to believe there had been an improvement in the reliability of news over time and, similar to Trump voters, were more likely to rate social media as the most reliable news platform.

Implications

Our results indicate that political ideology and partisanship are associated with how people consume news and their attitudes toward news but that demographic factors—such as age, gender, level of education, and employment status—are also important to news consumption choices. We consider several implications of our findings.

Consumption Choices and Social Media

Our results speak to the rising concerns about the increasing reliance of consumers on social media as a source of news. In this report, we provide insight into the degree to which consumers rely on social media for news and in what ways. About 30 percent of respondents reported relying on social media as their primary or secondary source of news, ranking it somewhere in the middle of news platforms in terms of use: It is neither the most used nor least used news platform. However, our data indicate that people rarely use social media as their sole source of news, and that those 30 percent of consumers who do rely heavily on social media for news are likely also using other news sources. These findings are consistent with research on media *complementarity*, the notion that different media platforms might serve different needs for information users.

News Consumption and Demographic Characteristics

Our results suggest that people use news media in different ways—relying on different types of news delivery platforms—and hold varying perceptions of reliability regarding those platforms and the news overall. Political partisanship explains some of these differences but certainly not all of them. Such factors as voting behaviors, age, gender, education, and marital status all play significant roles in explaining news consumption behaviors. As we note throughout this report, different news consumption profiles reflect aspects of an individual's demographics, such as living situation.

Our results reflect choices between platforms, not specific outlets, but these insights still have implications for efforts aimed at improving and supporting how people obtain and evaluate the news. Specifically, our analysis suggests that attention to reducing barriers to access, such as time limitations, might be as important as considering media literacy education as a way to provide information users with the skills they need to navigate a more complex online environment.

Perceptions of Media Reliability

Finally, we considered perceptions of media reliability and trust in the media. Our analysis confirms that many people are skeptical of the reliability of news overall, but it also shows that a small minority (particularly black and Hispanic individuals and those without a college degree) think that reliability is increasing. This underscores the importance of considering disaggregated data when studying media consumption and trust in the media. Attitudes about reliability also vary across different types of news platforms, with broadcast and cable news being considered the most-reliable sources, as previously discussed.

Our analysis also shows that attitudes toward the media are linked to consumption. For most users, reliability matters. News consumers tend to rely most heavily on the sources that they perceive as most reliable—though there are some exceptions, such as those who rely on other people and social media for news; some married people; and, unexpectedly, those who report believing that news is less reliable now than in the past. Skepticism about the reliability of the news does not necessarily increase an individual's likelihood of turning to news platforms they deem to be most reliable—in fact, we see the opposite.

That said, for all consumers, choices about media consumption are likely linked to individual characteristics, preferences, and behaviors. As a result, attempts to alter or improve relationships between media outlets and consumers are likely to require attention not just to the supply side of the information ecosystem (how media institutions operate and function) but also to the demand side and the ways in which people access news. Future work that explores news consumption in this more holistic way will be important as the informational ecosystem grows increasingly diverse and increasingly complex.

Acknowledgments

We would like to thank Michael D. Rich for his support and guidance throughout this process. We also thank David Grant, Karen Edwards, and Julie Newell for their assistance in developing and programming this survey. Wenjing Huang provided expert assistance on our data analysis. Shawn Smith provided valuable assistance as we prepared the final document. The authors also thank Gordon Lee for his assistance with our revisions.

As part of the RAND Corporation's quality assurance process, this report had three anonymous reviewers, one a RAND colleague and two external experts. We are grateful for their helpful feedback. Krishna Kumar and Rebecca Kilburn provided comments that allowed us to improve the document. Any errors are the authors' own.

Abbreviations

ABC	American Broadcasting Company
ALP	American Life Panel
CBS	Columbia Broadcasting Service
CNN	Cable News Network
EFA	exploratory factor analysis
MSNBC	Microsoft/National Broadcasting Company
NBC	National Broadcasting Company
OLS	ordinary least squares
PEPS	Presidential Election Panel Survey

CHAPTER ONE

Introduction

The news, in whatever form it comes, provides voters in a democracy with crucial information about domestic and international political events and policy issues that can inform their policy preferences and, ultimately, their voting decisions. Americans have an increasing number of news choices, in terms of both numbers of outlets and media platforms.[1] News can be found on more-traditional platforms (such as newspapers, radio, and television) or on newer platforms (such as digital journalism or social media posts). However, these options are varied in terms of content, tone, and intended audience. Social media, for instance, provides news in 280-character blocks (e.g., Twitter), whereas newspapers and some radio programs can do deep dives into specific topics. Similarly, the audience for cable television is very different from the audience for long-form print journalism.

In this increasingly diverse media ecosystem, news consumers' decisions can be based on any number of factors, such as availability, cost, time to consume, quality, or perceived reliability of a given outlet. Given this diversity, knowing something about what types of news people consume, how that news consumption is linked with demographic and political characteristics, and how perceived reliability of the consumed information factors into consumption patterns all can provide useful insights about both the overall market for news and the

---

[1] *News platforms* refers to different forms of media delivery—for example, websites, television, and print publications. We use the terms *sources* and *outlets* interchangeably to refer to the different components of each platform.

roles that such factors as partisanship, education, and race all play in news platform and outlet choices.

Objective of This Report

Using a nationally representative survey of English-speaking individuals ages 21 and older, this report addresses four main questions:

1. How do Americans get their news?
2. How are news consumption choices linked to demographic or political characteristics?
3. Do news consumers believe the reliability of news has changed, and which news platforms do they believe to be more or less reliable?
4. How is the perceived reliability of news associated with news consumption choices, such as platform choices and seeking out alternative viewpoints in the news?

Study Approach and Data

Our approaches to each of the study's four questions build on previous work (which we review in detail in subsequent sections) in several ways. First, we use rank-ordered data on a greater variety of news media platforms than has been used previously—consisting of print, broadcast television, cable television, radio, internet, social media, and in-person communication—combined with statistical methods to construct novel *news consumption profiles* characterizing the combinations through which news is accessed. Throughout this report, we describe how these news consumption profiles are linked to a variety of sociodemographic characteristics, individual behaviors, and attitudes.

Second, although perceptions of the relative reliability of news platforms have been examined previously, our study reflects what is, to our knowledge, the greatest variety of platforms considered simultaneously and one of the first attempts to develop such detailed descriptive assessments of the platforms used by individuals to obtain news. Although prior work has considered perceptions of several platforms at once, none has examined the full complement of different platforms featured in our analysis. We explore associations between perceived reliability and consumption decisions across platforms in a way that builds on previous analyses.

Finally, we examine what our analytical results suggest about *Truth Decay*, the phenomenon defined in a previous RAND Corporation report as the diminishing reliance on facts, data, and analysis in American public life.[2] As described in that report, the increasing diversity of the information ecosystem has both positive and negative implications. On one hand, having more options to choose from certainly empowers news consumers. On the other hand, an increase in different types and sources of information that might vary in their accuracy, their vulnerability to disinformation, and the extent to which they clearly distinguish between fact and opinion might make choices of what to consume more difficult. Our survey cannot explore all of these issues, but, in Chapter Four, we consider the implications of our survey results and analysis for Truth Decay— specifically whether people get their news from platforms they rate to be the most reliable, and whether they seek out diversity in the viewpoints of their news.

Our analysis and discussion rely on a survey conducted in February and March 2018 of 2,543 English-speaking members of the RAND American Life Panel (ALP) that asked about their perceptions of the reliability of various sources of news and about how they most frequently got their national and international news.[3] The sample for

---

[2] Jennifer Kavanagh and Michael D. Rich, *Truth Decay: An Initial Exploration of the Diminishing Role of Facts and Analysis in American Public Life*, Santa Monica, Calif.: RAND Corporation, RR-2314-RC, 2018. Previous RAND work defines *Truth Decay* as comprising four specific trends: an increasing disagreement about objective facts and analytical interpretations of data; blurring of the line between opinion and fact; the increasing relative volume of opinion (and its resulting influence) compared with facts; and declining trust in institutions, particularly those previously viewed as trusted sources of factual information.

[3] The ALP Omnibus survey did not have a Spanish language version, which is a limitation of our analysis. Note that the 2016 American Community Survey, conducted by the U.S. Census

this survey was randomly drawn from the larger ALP sample.[4] The ALP is a panel survey that consists of 6,000 U.S. respondents ages 18 and older who regularly take surveys over the internet.[5]

Since January 2006, the ALP has fielded more than 500 surveys on such topics as financial decisionmaking, the effect of political events on self-reported well-being, joint retirement decisions, health decisionmaking, Social Security knowledge and expectations, measurement of health utility, and voting preference in the presidential election. Data from all surveys are made publicly available to more than 600 clients and registered users from numerous institutions.

More than 100 research papers have been published using RAND ALP data. As with other surveys, we weight responses to ensure that our results are representative of the U.S. English-speaking population, matching to the U.S. Census Bureau's Current Population Survey.[6]

Because the ALP is a panel survey, we can construct a rich profile of individuals using past surveys—dating back to 2006 for some participants. This additional information about survey participants is one of the primary contributions of this study. We can connect news

---

Bureau, indicates that 91.5 percent of Americans speak English only or "speak English very well." Thus, results should not necessarily be interpreted as reflecting the 8.5 percent of the population that speaks English "less than 'very well.'" See U.S. Census, "Language Spoken at Home by Ability to Speak English for the Population 5 Years and over," webpage, 2017.

[4]   The survey was designed for a maximum number of 2,500 respondents because of budgeting constraints. A random sample of 3,357 were invited to take the survey in anticipation of a one-month field period; 2,570 had completed it after three weeks, and the survey was closed at that time.

[5]   ALP respondents are originally sampled by either random digit dial (landline and cell phone) or address; individuals cannot otherwise volunteer to participate. A further advantage over most other internet panels is that the respondents to the ALP need not have internet access when they are initially recruited (RAND provides laptops and internet subscriptions if needed), reducing an important source of bias. The panel is thus based on a probability sample of the U.S. population.

[6]   Complete technical details of the ALP, its recruitment, retention, and weighting procedures are available in Michael Pollard and Matthew D. Baird, *The RAND American Life Panel: Technical Description*, Santa Monica, Calif.: RAND Corporation, RR-1651, 2017; and at RAND Corporation, "Welcome to the ALP Data Pages," webpage, undated.

consumption today with not only political behaviors in past elections but also a variety of demographic characteristics in a way that existing work has not been able to do. This broader perspective provides us with some additional insights.

Other Surveys

As noted in later chapters, we have linked information where it was possible to do so from the news reliability survey to two other ALP surveys: the 2016 RAND Presidential Election Panel Survey (PEPS) and a 2018 survey on trust in institutions.[7] The PEPS data contain information on political partisanship and voting behavior during the 2016 presidential election, which supplements our questions about perceptions of broader sources of news. The trust in institutions data provide additional information on respondents' levels of trust in various types of media, which is used here to validate our measures of reliability. In Chapter Three, we provide information on the number of respondents and specific questions used in the surveys; we also discuss limitations of the analysis.

Contribution of This Report

In this report, we seek to build on past literature by providing a new perspective on questions that have been asked before and addressing some gaps in past literature, building on the following key insights from this past work. First, individuals typically use more than one type of media to get their news. Each news consumer, then, might have a unique basket of media platforms, and that mix might vary depending on the specific topic or types of sources available. Second, choices about which types of media to consume might be driven by individual characteristics, preferences, and market factors. Third, news consumption can be conceptualized as part of an individual's lifestyle, driven by

---

[7] Katherine Carman, "Well Being 496: Trust in Government," RAND American Life Panel, webpage, April 2018; Michael Pollard and Joshua Mendelsohn, *Methodology of the 2016 RAND Presidential Election Panel Survey (PEPS)*, Santa Monica, Calif.: RAND Corporation, RR-1460-RC/UCLA, 2016; and Michael Pollard and Joshua Mendelsohn, "RAND Kicks Off 2016 Presidential Election Panel Survey," *The RAND Blog*, January 27, 2016.

specific motivations and filling specific needs. (We review past work on news consumption decisions in detail in Chapter Two, summarizing several key insights and providing citations to the related work.)

Past research also considers the issue of trust in the media in an era of declining faith in the news overall, focusing on perceptions of the relative credibility of different news platforms, who is most likely to trust different outlets, and, in some cases, factors that lead to increased or diminished trust. Political partisanship, in particular, has been highlighted as having a strong role in determining overall views of media credibility for decades, with higher conservatism and Republican partisanship predicting greater mistrust. Age and education have also been identified as predictors of differing levels of trust in specific news platforms. Prior work suggests that both television and online news platforms are vying for the most trusted position. Finally, past research suggests that perceived credibility might not be all that closely related to consumption decisions. (We discuss this work in more detail in Chapter Two.)

This report advances past research in a few ways. First, building on the evidence that individuals use multiple news platforms in complementary ways, we use survey data to explore how people combine different types of information across an expanded array of options, identifying four news consumption profiles on which individuals rely to varying degrees. There have been previous efforts to do this,[8] and our analysis expands on this past work, providing richer detail and identifying the mix of different platforms and the demographic characteristics associated with each consumption type while also considering the degree of use of other types of platforms. Given that there is interest in how people consume news and concern about the quality of information available, a clearer and updated picture of the mix of sources used by different groups of people could be very informative and represents a key contribution of our report. A deeper analysis of who is most likely to consume which mix of different platforms is also valuable.

---

[8]   Kristin Van Damme, Cédric Courtois, Karel Verbrugge, and Lieven De Marez, "What's APPening to News? A Mixed-Method Audience-Centred Study on Mobile News Consumption," *Mobile Media & Communication*, Vol. 3, No. 2, 2015.

Second, although there has been significant research into both how people consume news and the extent to which people trust news, there has been less research that looks at the intersection of those topics. That is, do individuals with different news consumption profiles have different attitudes toward those media platforms and the reliability of that information? Do they have different consumption behaviors? The answers to these questions provide insights into the characteristics of different types of news consumers and can inform our understanding of when and why people do and do not trust media organizations. In addition to considering how news consumption profiles might relate to perceptions of media reliability, we also explore how perceptions of media reliability are linked to news consumption by comparing respondent reports about reliability with their actual consumption decisions.

Third, rather than asking about trust in media, we ask about *reliability*, seeking to understand the extent to which various types of media are dependable or produce dependable information. A comparison of these same respondents' reports about trust in media and their responses about reliability explores how the two concepts are related and ultimately indicates they are viewed similarly by news consumers. (We discuss this analytical choice in more detail in Chapter Three.)

Organization of This Report

In Chapter Two, we discuss what we know from past research about news consumption decisions, how individuals interact with news, and their attitudes toward news media. In Chapter Three, we discuss our analysis and results. We start with an assessment of the broad platforms from which people obtain their news and then identify four news consumption profiles using this information. We consider the question of perceived news reliability—how people rank different platforms and how perceived reliability is linked to news consumption choices. We then consider how willing people are to seek out alternative viewpoints and assess how that willingness varies across news consumption profile, partisanship, and other demographic characteristics. In the final chapter, we explore what the insights gained from these analyses suggest more generally about news consumption and how they might inform our understanding of Truth Decay. The three appendixes at the end of the report feature details of the statistical procedure used to identify news consumption profiles, descriptive statistics for the variables used in the report, and a supplementary analysis exploring the links between perceived reliability of news platforms and explicit trust in particular news platforms.

CHAPTER TWO

News Consumption and Attitudes Toward Media: Review of Past Work

There has already been significant research examining how people get news, the factors that shape their news consumption decisions, how news consumption fits into their lifestyles, and their general attitudes toward both media and news. In this chapter, we outline the key findings and insights of this past work, identify some existing limitations, and then discuss how our approach addresses some of these limitations.

What We Know About News Consumption

Research on patterns in news consumption explores not only the sources of news that people rely on but also the individual and environmental factors that influence news consumption decisions and how news consumption choices change over time as new types of media and more-diverse sources emerge.

Number of Sources: Displacement or Complementarity
Past research is clear that people typically use several different types of media and that this mix of platforms features both *traditional media* (print, radio, television) and *new media* (online news, social media). However, debate continues regarding whether different forms of news should be considered as complements or substitutes. A number of stud-

ies advance an argument of *complementarity*,[1] which argues that consumers are most likely to seek out a mix of different types (platforms) of news, perhaps to meet different needs, and behave no differently with new media than they do with traditional media.[2] Those who argue for complementarity suggest that consumers integrate new information sources into their existing media diet to complement their media consumption but might not eliminate older sources of information from their media consumption portfolio.

Exploring patterns of use, Van Damme et al. find some support for this argument, identifying three types of users: those who consume an extensive and diverse diet of news, those who consume primarily traditional sources of media with limited online content, and those who consume news less frequently and, when they do, rely on digital sources.[3] Similarly, Ahlers finds that 51 percent of those who get their news through online sources also relied on other sources.[4]

Ahlers' information is dated, but the pattern itself (of multichannel news consumption) remains relevant. Ahlers proposes a "consumer centric" model of news consumption, in which different users rely on different combinations of different platforms that are based on the users' own preferences and lifestyles.[5] Dutta-Bergman also finds evi-

---

[1]   Mohan J. Dutta-Bergman, "Complementarity in Consumption of News Types Across Traditional and New Media," *Journal of Broadcasting & Electronic Media*, Vol. 48, No. 1, 2004; Eugenia Mitchelstein and Pablo J. Boczkowski, "Online News Consumption Research: An Assessment of Past Work and an Agenda for the Future," *New Media & Society*, Vol. 12, No. 7, 2010.

[2]   Joey Ka-Ching Chan and Louis Leung, "Lifestyles, Reliance on Traditional News Media and Online News Adoption," *New Media & Society*, Vol. 7, No. 3, 2005; Steve Coffey and Horst Stipp, "The Interactions Between Computer and Television Usage," *Journal of Advertising Research*, Vol. 37, No. 2, 1997; Andrew J. Flanagin and Miriam J. Metzger, "Internet Use in the Contemporary Media Environment," *Human Communication Research*, Vol. 27, No. 1, 2001, pp. 153–181; Joseph M. Kayany and Paul Yelsma, "Displacement Effects of Online Media in the Socio-Technical Contexts of Households," *Journal of Broadcasting & Electronic Media*, Vol. 44, No. 2, 2000; and Mitchelstein and Boczkowski, 2010.

[3]   Van Damme et al., 2015.

[4]   Douglas Ahlers, "News Consumption and the New Electronic Media," *Harvard International Journal of Press/Politics*, Vol. 11, No. 1, 2006.

[5]   Ahlers, 2006.

dence to support this complementarity in consumption arguing that individuals rely on multiple different types of media to collect information on topics that are of interest to them.[6] Finally, Gaskins and Jerit specifically look at the replacement of traditional outlets by online sources; although they find some evidence of replacement, they note that the extent of replacement remains somewhat limited.[7] Of course, this might have changed in the years since the original study was conducted.

An alternative view is held by those who argue for *displacement*, which suggests that as new sources emerge, they replace or crowd out older and more-traditional sources of information. In this view, information consumers have only so much bandwidth for news, so attention devoted to one type of media will crowd out other media platforms. As evidence of this displacement theory, proponents point to the generally declining subscribership of major newspapers, especially among young readers, and the increasing number and diversity of those who consume news online.[8] Empirical tests that seek to validate the displacement theory find mixed results: Although displacement does occur for some forms of media and for some types of users, it does not appear to occur universally.[9] While the extent of displacement may be debated, there is clear evidence that it is occurring. A 2018 study, for instance,

---

[6] Dutta-Bergman, 2004.

[7] Benjamin Gaskins and Jennifer Jerit, "Internet News: Is It a Replacement for Traditional Media Outlets?" *International Journal of Press/Politics*, Vol. 17, No. 2, 2012, pp. 190–213.

[8] Matthew Gentzkow, "Valuing New Goods in a Model with Complementarity: Online Newspapers," *American Economic Review*, Vol. 97, No. 3, 2007; Barbara K. Kaye and Thomas J. Johnson, "From Here to Obscurity? Media Substitution Theory and Traditional Media in an Online World," *Journal of the American Society for Information Science and Technology*, Vol. 54, No. 3, 2003; and Carolyn Lin, Michael B. Salwen, Bruce Garrison, and Paul D. Driscoll, "Online News as a Functional Substitute for Offline News," in Michael B. Salwen, Bruce Garrison, and Paul D. Driscoll, eds., *Online News and the Public*, Mahwah, N.J.: Lawrence Erlbaum, 2005.

[9] Thomas F. Baldwin and Marianne Barrett, "Uses and Values for News on Cable Television," *Journal of Broadcasting and Electronic Media*, Vol. 36, No. 2, 1992; Stan J. Liebowitz and Alejandro Zentner, "Clash of the Titans: Does Internet Use Reduce Television Viewing?" *Review of Economics and Statistics*, Vol. 94, No. 1, 2012; and Laura Hazard Owen, "Here's Who Gets News from TV: The Elderly, Pew Finds (Again)," Neiman Lab, January 8, 2018.

found that young people shifted heavily into digital news consumption over the period from 1976 to 2016, suggesting a crowding out of traditional sources of media by social media for younger consumers.[10]

Survey data provide a mix of support for both the displacement and complementarity debates. On the side of complementarity, recent surveys by the Pew Research Center show that although an increasing number of Americans rely heavily on digital sources for their news— whether that is the online websites of newspapers, digital journalism sites, or social media—most continue to rely on traditional forms of media (such as newspapers, radio, or television) at the same time.[11]

Other patterns of media use appear to suggest some evidence for a displacement effect. While the number of Americans who seek news on social media and online has been increasing, the percentage relying on television and newspapers has experienced a long-term decline. Fifty-seven percent of Americans relied on television news in 2016; only 50 percent reported using television for news in 2017. Readership of print newspapers has fallen significantly, dropping to 31 million on weekdays (from a high of about 63.3 million in 1984) and 34 million on Sundays in 2017 (from a high of about 62.5 million in 1993).[12] As television and print journalism audiences decline, there has been a sharp increase in

---

[10] Jean M. Twenge, Gabrielle N. Martin, and Brian H. Spitzberg, "Trends in US Adolescents' Media Use, 1976–2016: The Rise of Digital Media, the Decline of TV, and the (Near) Demise of Print," *Psychology of Popular Media Culture*, August 2018. See also Oscar Westlund and Mathias A. Färdigh, "Accessing the News in an Age of Mobile Media: Tracing Displacing and Complementary Effects of Mobile News on Newspapers and Online News," *Mobile Media & Communication*, Vol. 3, No. 1, 2015.

[11] Amy Mitchell, Jeffrey Gottfried, Elisa Shearer, and Kristine Lu, *How Americans Encounter, Recall and Act Upon Digital News*, Washington, D.C.: Pew Research Center, February 9, 2017.

[12] Michael Barthel, "Newspapers Fact Sheet," webpage, Pew Research Center, June 13, 2018. An exception to the declining trends in more-conventional news sources is radio. The audience for radio broadcasting remains high—in 2017, 90 percent of Americans listened to some type of radio broadcast (both news and other programming). About 10 percent of radio audiences at any given point in the day are listening to news or talk radio. The online radio and podcast audience also has been growing steadily even in the face of new forms of media, running counter to some displacement arguments. In 2018, almost 50 percent of Americans reported having listened to a podcast at some point in their lives and 26 percent reported having listened to a podcast in the past month. This represents an increase of about

the use of online news sources—websites of newspapers, streaming news programs, and social media.[13] Importantly, recent surveys on media use show that the use of online sources of news is increasing among all demographic groups, including older Americans. In 2017, for instance, 55 percent of respondents older than 50 also reported using social media as a primary source of news.[14] These trends could be more consistent with a displacement argument, although the data provided do not explicitly reveal how much switching between media platforms is occurring (displacement) or what portion of observed trends is driven by new users entering the online market versus conventional media consumers opting out of news consumption more generally.

Past work exploring displacement and complementarity is useful for thinking about the relationships between different types of media and how individuals might optimize and select different platforms and sources to fill their information needs. Although debates about displacement and complementarity continue, past work suggests that individuals rely on multiple sources; even as an increasing number of consumers rely on online information and social media, use of more-traditional sources has not disappeared. Instead of thinking of consumers as "social media users" or "newspaper readers," it might be more accurate to think about each consumer as relying on a mix of different types of news for different types of subjects and existing in the spaces between news platforms. We will bring this set of expectations to our quantitative analysis.

Factors That Shape News Consumption Decisions

As the number of types of sources grows (along with the number of specific outlets within each of those types), an increasingly important and complex question focuses on which factors influence an individual's choices about which information sources to use. Past research identifies

---

2.5 times over the past decade. Elisa Shearer, "Audio and Podcasting Fact Sheet," webpage, Pew Research Center, July 12, 2018.

[13] Barthel, 2018.

[14] Elisa Shearer and Jeffrey Gottfried, "News Use Across Social Media Platforms 2017," webpage, Pew Research Center, September 7, 2017.

a variety of factors—such as demographic, social, and structural ones—that might influence an individual's news consumption attitudes.[15] Looking first at demographic characteristics, such factors as age, race, gender, and level of education have all been found to significantly influence decisions about information consumption.[16] For example, past research shows that men are more likely than women to engage with online news, particularly on social media. Younger consumers also appear more likely to rely on social media for news, although this might be a function of the amount of time they spend on the platform.[17] Consumers with higher incomes and more education also are more likely to be readers of online news.[18] In contrast, consumers of print newspapers tend to be older, more educated, more mobile, often urban, and more likely to be male, black, or unmarried.[19] Finally, it is worth noting that choices about news consumption also might reflect the interaction of individual characteristics and desired content. Although there is certainly overlap, different forms of media package news differently and so might appeal to different types of consumers.[20] These findings are also generally consistent with the Pew survey data already described.

---

[15] Alan M. Rubin, "Uses and Gratifications: An Evolving Perspective of Media Effects," in Robin L. Nabi and Mary Beth Oliver, eds., *The SAGE Handbook of Media Processes and Effects*, Thousand Oaks, Calif.: SAGE Publications, 2009; and Harsh Taneja, James G. Webster, Edward C. Malthouse, and Thomas B. Ksiazek, "Media Consumption Across Platforms: Identifying User-Defined Repertoires," *New Media and Society*, Vol. 14, No. 6, 2012.

[16] Angela M. Lee, "News Audiences Revisited: Theorizing the Link Between Audience Motivations and News Consumption," *Journal of Broadcasting & Electronic Media*, Vol. 57, No. 3, 2013; and Taneja et al., 2012.

[17] Carroll J. Glynn, Michael E. Huge, and Lindsay H. Hoffman, "All the News That's Fit to Post: A Profile of News Use on Social Networking Sites," *Computers in Human Behavior*, Vol. 28, No. 1, 2012; and Twenge, Martin, and Spitzberg, 2018.

[18] Guido H. Stempel and Thomas Hargrove, "Mass Media Audiences in a Changing Media Environment," *Journalism & Mass Communication Quarterly*, Vol. 73, No. 3, September 1996.

[19] Leo Bogart, "The Public's Use and Perception of Newspapers," *Public Opinion Quarterly*, Vol. 48, No. 4, January 1, 1984.

[20] Thomas E. Ruggiero, "Uses and Gratifications Theory in the 21st Century," *Mass Communication & Society*, Vol. 3, No. 1, 2001.

Other factors appear less significant to influencing choices of different information platforms. For example, there is strong evidence that partisanship and ideology affect choices of individual news outlets, but there is less evidence that ideological motivations are a significant driving factor in the choice of platform—newspaper, online sources, television, or radio—except through those platforms' relationships with desired media content and demographic characteristics. Work on selective exposure shows that the search for pro-attitudinal information (that which confirms one's beliefs or attitudes) guides decisions about which types of content to consume—for example, decisions on choosing media outlets, television programs, or specific journalists.[21] However, there is less evidence that partisan identification shapes choices regarding modes of media consumption once age and other demographic characteristics are accounted for.

Beyond these individual factors, previous research suggests that news consumption choices also are shaped by the structure of news markets. This research indicates that the concentration and diversity of available programming (local newspapers, local television channels, state and national news options) determine the options available and ultimately the news consumption behaviors of users. In other words, information supply likely plays as significant a role in information consumption decisions as do individual characteristics.[22] In emphasizing market structure, past work also underscores the importance of geography. Specifically, past research shows significant local and regional patterns in news consumption that extend beyond geographic clustering of individual characteristics and preferences.[23] Thus, it is not only

---

[21] R. Kelly Garrett and Natalie Jomini Stroud, "Partisan Paths to Exposure Diversity: Differences in Pro- and Counterattitudinal News Consumption," *Journal of Communication*, Vol. 64, No. 4, 2014; William Hart, Dolores Albarracín, Alice H. Eagly, Inge Brechan, Matthew J. Lindberg, and Lisa Merrill, "Feeling Validated Versus Being Correct: A Meta-Analysis of Selective Exposure to Information," *Psychological Bulletin*, Vol. 135, No. 4, 2009; and Natalie J. Stroud, *Niche News: The Politics of News Choice*, New York: Oxford University Press, 2011.

[22] Scott L. Althaus, Anne M. Cizmar, and James G. Gimpel, "Media Supply, Audience Demand, and the Geography of News Consumption in the United States," *Political Communication*, Vol. 26, No. 3, 2009.

[23] Althaus, Cizmar, and Gimpel, 2009.

individual preferences but also local and regional news markets and even an individual's own access to that market that determine the mix of sources that each individual relies on for news. Furthermore, local and regional market structure also relates directly to the amount of exposure an individual has to the news.[24]

Finally, in addition to individual and market characteristics, the lifestyle, general preferences, and motivations of news consumers appear to shape news consumption choices and patterns. Past research on the relationship between news consumption, motivation, and lifestyle suggests that we cannot consider news consumption choices in a vacuum but must explore the ways that news consumption interacts with an individual's other responsibilities, preferences, and motivations. Peters, for example, argues that news consumption is an activity that is attached to specific places and times, and so becomes part of an individual's everyday activity.[25] He notes that "the spaces of news consumption matter, and matter significantly, for how audiences experience journalism."[26] Different types of news and journalism might have different types of relationships with space and time. For example, research suggests that online media might be used in a greater diversity of places and in shorter periods of time than other forms of media, which might more often be consumed in the same places and same times.[27]

Other theories about news consumption decisions suggest that these choices are based on individual information needs and the search for gratification.[28] In other words, individuals will rely on informa-

---

[24] Althaus, Cizmar, and Gimpel, 2009.

[25] Chris Peters, "Journalism to Go," *Journalism Studies*, Vol. 13, Nos. 5–6, 2012.

[26] Peters, 2012, p. 696.

[27] Taneja et al., 2012; and Cornelia Wolf and Anna Schnauber, "News Consumption in the Mobile Era," *Digital Journalism*, Vol. 3, No. 5, 2015.

[28] Jay G. Blumler and Elihu Katz, *The Uses of Mass Communications*, Beverly Hills, Calif.: Sage Publications, 1974; Edgar Huang, "The Causes of Youths' Low News Consumption and Strategies for Making Youths Happy News Consumers," *Convergence: The International Journal of Research into New Media Technologies*, Vol. 15, No. 1, 2009; Marina Krcmar and Yuliya Strizhakova, "Uses and Gratifications as Media Choice," in Tilo Hartmann, ed., *Media Choice: A Theoretical and Empirical Overview*, New York: Routledge, 2009; Lee,

tion sources providing them with information they need or want or affording them the most gratification. There are many possible motivations that might drive individuals in their information consumption decisions. Previous research suggests that users might seek information, answers to questions, a diversion from boredom, comfort or confirmation, entertainment, or social connection through their information consumption.[29] A framework by Lee,[30] for example, proposes four main sets of motivations guiding news consumption decisions: (1) entertainment;[31] (2) ideologically driven choices, rooted in the search for confirmatory information;[32] (3) socially motivated consumption;[33] and (4) information seeking.[34] Evaluating the prevalence of these four motivations, Lee finds that people are most likely to be motivated by the search for information and least likely to seek out news for reasons related to ideology and opinion.[35] However, it is likely that these two motivations are intertwined for many people. Lee also notes that news

---

2013; and Carolyn Lin, "Modeling the Gratification-Seeking Process of Television Viewing," *Human Communication Research*, Vol. 20, No. 2, 1993.

[29] Flanagin and Metzger, 2001; Lee, 2013; and Zizi Papacharissi and Alan M. Rubin, "Predictors of Internet Use," *Journal of Broadcasting & Electronic Media*, Vol. 44, No. 2, 2000.

[30] Lee, 2013.

[31] Jay D. Hmielowski, R. Lance Holbert, and Jayeon Lee, "Predicting the Consumption of Political TV Satire: Affinity for Political Humor, *The Daily Show*, and *The Colbert Report*," *Communication Monographs*, Vol. 78, No. 1, 2011.

[32] R. Kelly Garrett, "Echo Chambers Online? Politically Motivated Selective Exposure Among Internet News Users," *Journal of Computer-Mediated Communication*, Vol. 14, No. 2, 2009; and Shanto Iyengar and Kyu S. Hahn, "Red Media, Blue Media: Evidence of Ideological Selectivity in Media Use," *Journal of Communication*, Vol. 5, 2009.

[33] Vivian B. Martin, "Attending the News: A Grounded Theory About a Daily Regimen," *Journalism*, Vol. 9, No. 1, 2008; Michele Weldon, *Everyman News: The Changing American Front Page*, Columbia, Mo.: University of Missouri Press, 2008.

[34] Matthias R. Hastall, "Information Utility as Determinant of Media Choices," in Tilo Hartmann, ed., *Media Choice: A Theoretical and Empirical Overview*, New York: Routledge, 2009; and Pamela J. Shoemaker, "Hardwired for News: Using Biological and Cultural Evolution to Explain Surveillance Function," *Journal of Communication*, Vol. 46, No. 3, 1996.

[35] Lee, 2013.

consumption is motivated by multiple and overlapping motivations rather than just one.

Another body of related research has focused on identifying media "repertoires," or multiplatform sets of news sources that media users construct to meet their many different needs and preferences. Repertoires might be multiple outlets, channels, forms of media, and even means of delivery (e.g., radio via car stereo or streaming).[36] The concept of repertoires underscores the notion that individuals rely on many sources of media simultaneously and that they are able to update their media diet as media options become more diverse. We will return to the concept of media repertoires in the next chapter.

The diversity of motivations becomes more important as news consumers have access to an increasing diversity of types of information, with important implications for levels of political knowledge across the electorate. Prior shows that as content becomes more diverse, those seeking detailed political information and those seeking entertainment are each able to find the information that they are most interested in.[37] As this sorting process occurs, those with political interest become increasingly versed in political affairs; those without this interest fall further and further behind in political knowledge. From the perspective of understanding and studying news consumption patterns, this research suggests that not only do individuals get information through different types of platforms, they also likely get different types of information and acquire different types of knowledge.[38]

How Attitudes Toward Media and News Vary

Just as individuals vary in their choices of modes of information consumption, so do they vary significantly in their attitudes toward the

---

[36] Taneja et al., 2012.

[37] Markus Prior, "News vs. Entertainment: How Increasing Media Choice Widens Gaps in Political Knowledge and Turnout," *American Journal of Political Science*, Vol. 49, No. 3, July 2005.

[38] Prior, 2005.

news media, particularly their trust in media institutions and journalists and their beliefs about the credibility or reliability of the information provided by these information sources.

As noted, trust in media in the United States tends to be low in aggregate terms. Audience trust in news media has been in a long decline from a relative high in the 1970s.[39] In fact, a 2018 Pew survey suggests that American respondents consider the media to be significantly less fair and less accurate than do respondents in other countries. Only 47 percent of Americans believe that the news media report issues fairly; only 56 percent believe the media report issues accurately. Compare this with Canada, where 73 and 78 percent of respondents, respectively, hold these attitudes toward media's fairness and accuracy.[40] Americans want an independent and unbiased media and strongly believe that this is important for democracy, but less than one-half can name a source they consider objective.[41] This could mean that there are few objective sources available, that many consumers simply perceive more sources to be biased, or that individuals tend to remember and fixate on those that are generally not objective.

There are many reasons why trust in media appears to be low. High-profile mistakes and concern about false information online and in print and television journalism might be one reason. For example, more than 50 percent of consumers say they believe that online news sources report false information and 70 percent report feeling that social media companies are not doing enough to stop the spread of false information.[42] A majority also say they believe that media compa-

---

[39] Stephen Earl, Staci L. Rhine, and Richard S. Flickinger, "Assessing Americans' Opinions About the News Media's Fairness in 1996 and 1998," *Political Communication*, Vol. 18, No. 2, 2001; and David A. Jones, "Why Americans Don't Trust the Media: A Preliminary Analysis," *Harvard International Journal of Press/Politics*, Vol. 9, No. 2, 2004.

[40] Amy Mitchell, Katie Simmons, Katerina Eva Matsa, and Laura Silver, "Publics Globally Want Unbiased News Coverage, but Are Divided on Whether Their News Media Deliver," Pew Research Center, January 11, 2018.

[41] Knight Foundation and Trust, Media and Democracy, "10 Reasons Why American Trust in the Media Is at an All-Time Low," *Medium*, January 15, 2018.

[42] Christine Schmidt, "Planted Stories? Fake News as Editorial Decisions? Trump or CNN? A Poll Examines the Public's Trust of Mainstream Media," Neiman Lab, April 3, 2018.

nies play a role in the problem not only by printing false information but also because of the stories they choose to print.[43] About 70 percent of news consumers say publication of false information is intentional sometimes or often, although this number is significantly higher for Republicans (92 percent) than Democrats (53 percent).[44] An increasing number of sources might also be eroding trust in news and confusing consumers seeking fact-based information.[45]

Attitudes toward the media are heavily affected by political attitudes and partisanship in the United States. Consistently across surveys, Republicans tend to be less trusting of the media and to rate media coverage more negatively than Democrats, who view the media more positively in general.[46] More than one-half of Democrats view the news media favorably; almost 70 percent of Republicans have an unfavorable view.[47] A recent study of trust in the media conducted by the Knight Foundation in cooperation with Gallup found that news consumers significantly reduce their perception of the trustworthiness of news on learning that it comes from a source on the other side of the political aisle (e.g., Fox News for Democrats or MSNBC for Republicans).[48] Past research also has found that the link between partisanship and trust in media might reflect the effect of perceived bias; individuals who perceive bias in media content tend to report lower levels of trust in media as a result.[49] Importantly, this partisan divide is not new to this decade. Research on trust in the media has consistently

---

[43] Schmidt, 2018.

[44] Sara Fischer, "92% of Republicans Think Media Intentionally Reports Fake News," *Axios*, June 27, 2018.

[45] Knight Foundation and Trust, Media and Democracy, 2018.

[46] Albert C. Gunther, "Biased Press or Biased Public?" *Public Opinion Quarterly*, Vol. 56, No. 2, 1992; Jones, 2004; and Tien-Tsun Lee, "Why They Don't Trust the Media: An Examination of Factors Predicting Trust," *American Behavioral Scientist*, Vol. 54, No. 1, 2010.

[47] Knight Foundation and Trust, Media and Democracy, 2018.

[48] Knight Foundation, *An Online Experimental Platform to Assess Trust in the Media*, Miami, Fla., July 18, 2018.

[49] Lee, 2010.

found that those with conservative political views tend to have lower trust in the media than other respondents.[50] More generally, previous work has found that trust in government and in the media are often closely related: Individuals who have low trust in government also tend to have lower trust in the media.[51]

Individuals rate the credibility of specific methods or platforms of news provision differently, although methods of assessing these rankings vary. In the earliest studies, newspapers were rated as more credible than television or radio.[52] But beginning in the 1960s and lasting through the end of the century, television steadily gained as the most credible source, followed by newspapers and radio.[53]

With the growth in internet-based news dissemination, there have been inconsistent reports of the perceived credibility of online news sources: Some studies identify online news as being considered more credible than television or newspapers;[54] others report it to be viewed as less credible.[55] Some of this inconsistency might reflect the fact that individuals appear to judge the credibility of different platforms using different criteria. For instance, one study found that news-

---

[50] Jones, 2004.

[51] Stephen Earl Bennett, Staci L. Rhine, Richard S. Flickinger, and Linda L. M. Bennett, "'Video Malaise' Revisited: Public Trust in the Media and Government," *Harvard International Journal of Press/Politics*, Vol. 4, No. 4, 1999; Jones, 2004.

[52] Matthias Kohring and Jörg Matthes, "Trust in News Media: Development and Validation of a Multidimensional Scale," *Communication Research*, Vol. 34, No. 2, 2007.

[53] Richard F. Carter and Bradley S. Greenberg, "Newspaper or Television: Which Do You Believe?" *Journalism Quarterly*, Vol. 42, No. 1, 1965; Cecilie Gaziano and Kristin McGrath, "Measuring the Concept of Credibility," *Journalism Quarterly*, Vol. 63, No. 3, 1986; Kohring and Matthes, 2007; and Bruce H. Westley and Werner J. Severin, "Some Correlates of Media Credibility," *Journalism Quarterly*, Vol. 41, No. 3, 1964.

[54] Thomas J. Johnson and Barbara K. Kaye, "Cruising Is Believing? Comparing Internet and Traditional Sources on Media Credibility Measures," *Journalism & Mass Communication Quarterly*, Vol. 75, No. 2, 1998; and Jenn Burleson Mackay and Wilson Lowrey, "The Credibility Divide: Reader Trust of Online Newspapers and Blogs," *Journal of Media Sociology*, Vol. 3, Nos. 1–4, 2011.

[55] Spiro Kiousis, "Public Trust of Mistrust? Perceptions of Media Credibility in the Information Age," *Mass Communication & Society*, Vol. 4, No. 4, 2001; and Pew Research Center, *One-in-Ten Voters Online for Campaign '96*, Washington, D.C., December 16, 1996.

papers were judged as an institution, whereas television news sources are often judged based on the credibility of individual reporters who use images and other evidence to convince viewers of their reliability.[56]

Focus has tended to be on the relative credibility of various news platforms or how perceptions of credibility or trust in types of news media relate to the use of those types of media. But a handful of previous studies explicitly focused on identifying background factors that are associated with perceptions of the relative credibility of specific news platforms. Bucy noted that younger, college-educated individuals said they believed television and online news sources were credible overall more often than older individuals did, although older individuals rated online news as more credible than television (whereas younger people rated television as more credible).[57]

Research has shown that perceptions of overall news media credibility are not necessarily correlated with overall frequency of news consumption.[58] Past work does suggest, however, that perceived credibility might be associated with news consumption decisions—for choices between platforms and between outlets.[59] Although there are likely exceptions, people tend to choose to use sources of news they trust over sources they distrust.[60] Looking specifically at cable news, for example,

---

[56] John Newhagen and Clifford Nass, "Differential Criteria for Evaluating Credibility of Newspapers and TV News," *Journalism Quarterly*, Vol. 66, No. 2, 1989.

[57] Erik P. Bucy, "Media Credibility Reconsidered: Synergy Effects Between On-Air and Online News," *Journalism and Mass Communication Quarterly*, Vol. 80, No. 2, 2003.

[58] Wayne Wanta and Yu-Wei Hu, "The Effects of Credibility, Reliance, and Exposure on Media Agenda-Setting: A Path Analysis Model," *Journalism Quarterly*, Vol. 71, No. 1, 1994.

[59] Ronald J. Faber, Stephen D. Reese, and Leslie H. Steeves, "Spending Time with the News Media: The Relationship Between Reliance and Use," *Journal of Broadcasting and Electronic Media*, Vol. 29, No. 4, 1985; and Wanta and Hu, 1994.

[60] Robert P. Hawkins, Suzanne Pingree, Jacqueline Hitchon, Bradley W. Gorham, Prathna Kannaovakun, Eileen Gilligan, Barry Radler, Gudbjorg H. Kolbeins, and Toni Schmidt, "Predicting Selection and Activity in Television Genre Viewing," *Media Psychology*, Vol. 3, No. 3, 2001; Nikolaus G. Jakob, "No Alternatives? The Relationship Between Perceived Media Dependency, Use of Alternative Information Sources, and General Trust in Mass Media," *International Journal of Communication*, Vol. 4, 2010; Natalie Jomini Stroud and Jae Kook Lee, "Perceptions of Cable News Credibility," *Mass Communication and Society*, Vol. 16, No. 1, 2013; Yariv Tsfati and Joseph N. Cappella, "Do People Watch What They Do Not

Stroud and Lee show that perceived credibility of specific outlets is an important factor in explaining the relationship between political attitudes and cable news consumption choices.[61] One question that is less fully explored by past work, however, is how perceived credibility interacts with demographic and political characteristics to shape cross-platform trade-offs for news consumers in an increasingly diverse news environment. We explore this question and others in our analyses in the next chapter.

Trust? Exploring the Association Between News Media Skepticism and Exposure," *Communication Research*, Vol. 30, No. 5, 2003; and Lawrence R. Wheeless, "The Effects of Attitude, Credibility, and Homophily on Selective Exposure to Information," *Speech Monographs*, Vol. 41, 1974, pp. 329–338.

[61] Stroud and Lee, 2013.

CHAPTER THREE

News That People Consume: News Consumption Profiles

As noted in the previous chapter, individuals vary in the number and types of news sources that they consume. Some people might read hours of news articles per day, others might listen to a single podcast, and still others might rely on social media or conversations with friends. This chapter directly explores the ways in which people obtain their news and derives news consumption profiles that describe how heavily individuals rely on each of four typical avenues through which people get their news. We also investigate how political partisanship—in terms of both ideology and voting behavior—is linked to news consumption and attitudes about the news. Our findings are generally consistent with previous studies but offer additional nuance into how news consumption and reliance on certain news platforms might reflect not only such basic demographic characteristics as age and race but also such broader contextual factors as marital and employment status.

How People Get Their News

We first asked people to tell us how they got most of their national and international news, ranking the top four platforms in the order they used them. We offered them several major media categories: print publications (e.g., newspapers and news magazines), broadcast television (e.g., ABC, NBC, CBS), cable television (e.g., CNN, Fox, MSNBC), radio news programs (including streaming; e.g., Sirius), online news and newspaper websites (e.g., The Bill, Breitbart, Huffington Post, nytimes.com), social media (e.g., Facebook, Twitter), and in-person communication (e.g., friends, family, personal networks at such places as work or church).[1]

The most common response for the primary news platform was broadcast television, closely followed by online sources (Figure 3.1). Cable television and social media were the second most-common platforms, with radio, print, and in-person communication being less common as primary platforms. When the first and second most-used platforms were combined, the pattern generally remained the same (Figure 3.2). The in-person platform was the least common choice among respondents choosing their most used source of news, but it was a popular second choice, which moved it up in the rankings to the point where it was ultimately listed among the top two platforms in our survey, above print or radio.

The data show that user preference for print journalism is less common than for television, digital and online journalism, and social

Figure 3.1
Respondents' Most Used News Source

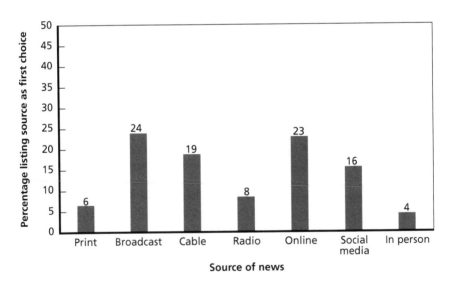

---

[1]   Although comparing differences within these broad platforms would be helpful (e.g., newspapers versus magazines within print, or even specific outlets or sources of print news), the broader-channel comparison is more suitable for an exploratory study such as this.

Figure 3.2
Respondent's Top Two Most-Used News Sources

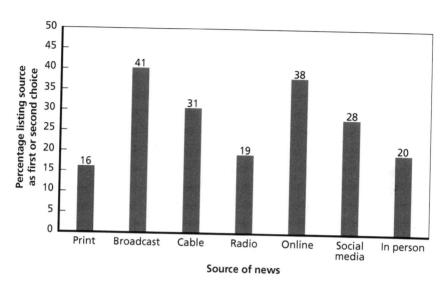

media as the primary source of news. On the other hand, despite concern about Americans relying solely on social media for news,[2] our data show that only about 15 percent rely on it as a first choice and 14 percent select it as a second choice. Finally, the survey indicates that about one in five Americans relies on other people (e.g., friends, family, social networks) as their first or second choice for news. This reinforces the role that social networks play in spreading news.

News Consumption Profiles

We can push the data further to get more-detailed patterns of the ways that people consume news. To better understand these patterns, we used a statistical technique known as factor analysis to identify four underlying common combinations of ranked news platforms used by the people in our survey and to determine how strongly each of these

2   Katerina Eva Matsa and Elisa Shearer, "News Use Across Social Media Platforms 2018," webpage, Pew Research Center, September 10, 2018.

underlying combinations fits each respondent.[3] News consumption profiles, as we define them here, are similar to the media repertoires described in Chapter Two, but our approach is distinct from this past work both in our use of ranked data and in our focus at the platform level (rather than the channel or outlet level).[4]

Identification of the four factors and how individuals scored on each of them were determined based on the rank order that individuals provided for the top four news platforms they used. Individuals scored higher on factors that matched their own ranking patterns and lower on factors that did not match. For example, someone who reported that his or her most commonly used platforms (in order) were online, print news, broadcast television, and radio would, in the factor analysis, score highest on online, followed by print/broadcast and radio, with the social media/in-person category having the lowest score. The factor analysis process allows us to use these different scores to sort respondents into groups with similar news consumption use habits, which we call *news consumption profiles.*

Our analysis identified four news consumption profiles comprising the best description of the data: social media and in-person contact,[5] print and broadcast television, radio, and online. Note that this indicates that social media and in-person sources were commonly closely ranked, as were print and broadcast television, leading those platform combinations to be combined as single news consumption profiles.

A closer look at the data provides additional insight into these groups. Although cable television is a relatively common method of

---

[3] Broadly, *factor analysis* is a statistical technique that is used to reduce data to a smaller set of summary variables (factors) and to explore their underlying structure. We initially used exploratory factor analysis (EFA) to derive the number of underlying factors, and then used confirmatory factor analysis (CFA) to fit the hypothesized factor structure to the data (respondents). Factor scores for each dimension of the consumption profile have a mean of 0 and a standard deviation of 1 for the entire sample, which means individuals can have positive or negative values on each dimension. Complete details of the factor analysis procedures are provided in Appendix A.

[4] Taneja et al., 2012.

[5] This grouping could also be described as "peer-to-peer news," which is an appropriate way to think of these platforms. We retain "social media and in-person" for clarity.

obtaining news, it was not identified as a significant consumption profile factor in the final or even preliminary factor analysis. This suggests that although cable news consumption is relatively ubiquitous, it does not provide a distinct news consumption signature on its own in our data. Broadly, an individual's consumption profile factor score places him or her most strongly in one category, but he or she also might have characteristics of other categories. Although each individual tends to score highly on one of the consumption profile dimensions, he or she might also use other news platforms frequently; these sources are likely to play a smaller role in that person's overall news consumption, and accordingly are given lower scores on those dimensions. If platforms were not highly used or not used at all by individuals, factor scores for those profile dimensions are negative. Note that this also means that because cable television does not appear as one of the consumption profile dimensions, for people who do rely heavily and nearly exclusively on cable television, factor scores for all consumption profile factors are negative, indicative of the poor match between those profiles and the respondent's cable news consumption pattern.

The news consumption profiles exemplify the concept of media repertoires used by individuals to combine multiple types of news sources simultaneously to various degrees. The concepts of complementarity and displacement are less directly relevant but still provide a way of thinking about how people develop their own media repertoires and how sources within an individual's repertoire might interact.

Demographic Characteristics of News Consumption Profiles

We found that each of our four news consumption profiles was also demographically distinct. Demographic characteristics of respondents in each news consumption profile are described in Tables 3.1 and 3.2. Table 3.1 presents the results of a series of ordinary least squares (OLS) regressions predicting each respondent's factor score: Model 1 uses a set of sociodemographic variables (age, sex [male/female], race, level of education, household income, marital status, presence of children in the household, and retirement status); Model 2 also considers partisanship variables. Table 3.2 presents a verbal interpretation of the results of Model 1 in Table 3.1. Descriptive statistics (means, proportions, and

Table 3.1
Characteristics Associated with News Consumption Profile Factors (OLS Coefficients)

Characteristic	Social Media/In-Person		Print/Broadcast		Radio		Online	
	Model 1	Model 2	Model 1	Model 2	Model 1	Model 2	Model 1	Model 2
Age	-0.019***	-0.020***	0.002	0.007*	0.000	0.001	-0.015***	-0.016***
Male	-0.320***	-0.355***	0.072	0.015	0.125*	0.168*	0.126*	0.152*
Black	-0.256**	-0.099	0.038	0.037	-0.062	-0.024	-0.212*	-0.327*
Hispanic	-0.210*	-0.154	-0.201†	-0.209	-0.026	-0.004	-0.106	-0.026
Other race	-0.232	-0.356	-0.073	0.069	0.116	0.143	-0.011	-0.030
College	-0.163*	-0.164*	0.100	0.106	0.112†	0.141†	0.212**	0.180*
Income	-0.001	-0.001*	0.000	-0.001	0.000	0.000	-0.001*	0.001†
Married	-0.073	-0.045	-0.118	-0.145†	0.056	0.034	-0.061	-0.065
Any children	-0.002	0.033	-0.021	-0.016	-0.005	0.009	0.026	0.041
Retired	-0.043	-0.053	0.069	-0.004	-0.328***	-0.278**	-0.020	0.032
News reliability overall (compared with no change)								
Less reliable now		-0.025		0.021		0.041		0.117
More reliable now		-0.183†		-0.125		-0.130		-0.293***
Partisanship								
Conservatism		0.010		0.036		0.016		-0.067*
Voted for Trump		0.069		-0.307**		-0.046		-0.169†
Voted for someone other than Trump or Clinton		0.263*		-0.118		0.245		-0.023
Did not vote		-0.147		-0.048		0.091		0.152

NOTE: Throughout this report, regression models without partisanship have N = 2,649, and with partisanship N = 2,030. † p < 0.10; * p < 0.05; ** p < 0.01; *** p < 0.001.

Table 3.2
Summary of Media Consumption Profile Characteristics: Demographics Only

Demographics	Social Media/ In-Person	Print/ Broadcast	Radio	Online
Age	Younger	N/A	N/A	Younger
Gender	Female	N/A	Male	Male
Race/ethnicity	White	Non-Hispanic	N/A	Not black
Educational attainment	No college degree	N/A	College degree	College degree
Income	N/A	N/A	N/A	Lower income
Married	N/A	N/A	N/A	N/A
Retired or working	N/A	N/A	Working	N/A

NOTE: N/A indicates that variables were not significantly associated with news consumption profiles in the OLS regressions.

standard deviations) for the demographic and other variables used in this study are presented in Appendix B.

People who reported primarily getting their news from social media and in-person contacts tended to be younger, female, and white (versus black or Hispanic), and they tended to have less education than a college degree. People who reported mostly getting their news through the print and broadcast television platforms were less likely to be Hispanic. Radio consumers were significantly more likely to be male, less likely to be retired, and marginally significantly more likely to have a college degree. Online news consumers were significantly younger; more likely to be male, have a college degree, and have lower income; and less likely to be black.

Political Characteristics and News Consumption Profiles

We know from previous research that political beliefs and partisanship also affect news consumption decisions. To explore the relationship between news consumption profiles and political characteristics, we expanded our second set of analyses to factor in two political variables taken from the PEPS conducted in 2016. Using the combined data, we can expand our understanding of media consumption patterns. The PEPS data feature information on an individual's political ideology (along a 5-point scale, ranging from 1 = "very liberal" to 5 = "very conservative") and who they voted for in the 2016 presidential election, if they voted (self-reported).[6] We were able to link 82 percent of our 2018 sample to the earlier PEPS sample's information (N = 2,181) based on the overlap between the two survey samples within the ALP overall.[7] Table 3.3 presents descriptive results of the analysis, including the political variables, taken from Model 2 of Table 3.1. Comparisons are made with people who voted for Clinton because that was the most commonly reported behavior in the sample (41.2 percent of respon-

Table 3.3
Summary of Media Consumption Profile Characteristics (Considering Partisanship)

Demographics	Social Media/In-Person	Print/Broadcast	Radio	Online
Age	Younger	Older	N/A	Younger
Gender	Female	N/A	Male	Male
Race or ethnicity	N/A	N/A	N/A	Not black
Educational attainment	No college degree	N/A	College degree	College degree
Income	Lower income	N/A	N/A	Higher income
Married	N/A	Not married	N/A	N/A
Retired or working	N/A	N/A	Working	N/A
Partisanship				
Political ideology	N/A	N/A	N/A	More liberal
Vote choice in 2016	Most likely to have voted for someone other than Clinton or Trump	Most likely to have voted for Clinton	N/A	Most likely to have voted for Clinton

NOTE: N/A indicates that variables were not significantly associated with news consumption profile factors in the OLS regressions.

---

[6]   The correlation between political ideology and voting for Donald Trump or Hillary Clinton was moderate at 0.57 and at −0.056, respectively; however, the results were not substantively different when models were run with each aspect of partisanship separately.

[7]   Note that restricting analyses to only those who could be matched to the PEPS provides similar results throughout the analyses to analyses that do not link to the PEPS.

dents, followed by 35.1 percent who voted for Trump) and because having the largest group as the referent category simplifies the analysis and interpretation. When reporting these results, however, we consider comparisons of different groups of voters (those who voted for Clinton, those who voted for Trump, those who voted for someone else, and those who did not vote). We do not report every comparison in every case; we emphasize those comparisons that are statistically significant and meaningful while pointing out key areas where no clear relationship exists.

We find that political beliefs and voting behavior matter, but not as much as might be expected based on previous work and popular news coverage. First, compared with those who voted for Clinton in 2016, respondents who reported voting for Trump were significantly less likely to score as highly on the print/broadcast news consumption profile. However, Trump voters were no more or less likely to score differently on any of the other news consumption profiles. Second, those who voted for someone other than Trump or Clinton were more likely than those who voted for Clinton to score highly on the social media/in-person profile. Third, respondents who rated their political ideology as more conservative were somewhat less likely to be in the online group (and those who self-identified as liberals slightly more likely), although this result is both substantively smaller and marginally statistically significant. The addition of the two political variables generally does not substantially alter the previous findings related to the demographics of the news consumption profiles. Exceptions are that when political characteristics are also considered, those who were married were less likely to score highly in the print/ broadcast consumption profile, older individuals were more likely to score highly in the print/broadcast profile, and low income was associated with higher scores on the social media/in-person profile.

Taken together, older individuals were more likely to report getting their news using more-traditional platforms—print and broadcast television—than younger individuals. Younger respondents were more likely to report getting their news from social media/in-person sources or online. Women were more likely to report getting their news through more-social means (social media or in person). Non-Hispanic white respondents were generally more likely than others to report relying heavily on social media/in-person sources and online platforms for obtaining their news.

Attitudes About News Reliability

Perceptions of Whether News Has Become More or Less Reliable

We next investigate whether there are links between the ways in which people access news and their perceptions of news reliability. That is, are there consistent differences in perceptions of the reliability of news across media consumption profiles? In addition to reporting which sources they use most often, respondents were asked to rank "which source provides the most-reliable information, in your opinion" and whether they "find the news you currently receive . . ." to be "more or less reliable . . . than in the past" (or about the same). We asked about reliability of information, rather than trust, because we wanted to assess the degree to which respondents felt that they could rely or consistently depend on a given news platform and its coverage to provide accurate information. The term *reliability* captures this consistent dependability more directly than the word *trust* and places the emphasis on news provided by a media source, which was what we were most interested in, rather than on the institution itself. We note that past research on perceived media credibility or trust has tended to use the terms interchangeably but has also demonstrated that the various components of media trust (such as accuracy, fairness, unbiasedness, trustworthiness, reliability) load together well and are empirically inseparable.[8] We explore the relationship between the concepts of reliability and trust further in a subsequent section, and we show that results are qualitatively the same using "reliability" or "trust." To do so, we added

---

[8] Richard Fletcher and Sora Park "The Impact of Trust in the News Media on Online News Consumption and Participation," *Digital Journalism*, Vol. 5, No. 10, 2017; Gaziano, and McGrath, 1986; Philip Meyer, "Defining and Measuring Credibility of Newspapers: Developing an Index," *Journalism Quarterly*, Vol. 65, No. 3, 1988; Tsfati and Cappella, 2003; Mark Douglas West, "Validating a Scale for the Measurement of Credibility: A Covariance Structure Modeling Approach," *Journalism Quarterly*, Vol. 71, No. 1, 1994.

consideration of level of trust toward a variety of news platforms from a separate ALP survey. Further details of the comparison are presented in Appendix C, but the results show that, conceptually, trust and reliability are closely related for consumers when assessing various news platforms. Furthermore, just as perceived reliability is associated with news consumption choices, a respondent's trust in various news platforms is also associated with information use habits.

General perceptions about the reliability of the news overall among the survey respondents reflected a substantial amount of pessimism. Although 44 percent reported that they believed "the news is as reliable now as in the past," nearly the same amount—41 percent—reported a belief that the news has become less reliable. A minority (15 percent) said that they believed that the news is more reliable now than in the past. There are systematic differences in perceptions based on both demographic and political characteristics (Tables 3.4 and 3.5). Table 3.4 presents the relative risk ratios derived from a multinomial logit regression, comparing those reporting that news is "more reliable now" and those reporting that the news is "less reliable now" to those reporting that the news is "as reliable now." Values greater than 1 indicate factors associated with increased likelihood of the belief (compared with "as reliable now"); values less than 1 identify characteristics that are associated with a reduced likelihood of the belief. Table 3.5 presents a verbal summary of the results in Table 3.4.

Without attention to partisanship (Model 1 in Table 3.4), respondents who were white, male, or retired or who had higher incomes or less than a college education were significantly more likely to believe the news is less reliable now (compared with as reliable as in the past). Conversely, women, racial or ethnic minorities, and those without college degrees were significantly more likely to say they believed that the news is more reliable now than in the past. Finally, we sought to explore the relationship between news consumption profiles and perceptions of reliability. We found that those who were more likely to use social media/in-person sources and online news platforms to get their news were less likely to feel that news had become more reliable, but no profile was associated with perceptions of reductions in reliability.

Table 3.4
Characteristics Associated with Perceptions of News Reliability (Relative Risk Ratios from Multinomial Logistic Regression)

	More Reliable Now		Less Reliable Now		As Reliable Now
Demographics	Model 1	Model 2	Model 1	Model 2	(Reference)
Age	1.003	0.996	0.992	0.988	
Male	0.632*	0.799	1.446*	1.323	
Black	1.959*	2.277*	0.393**	0.824	
Hispanic	2.204**	2.419**	0.634†	0.872	
Other race	1.078	0.695	0.699	0.740	
College	0.613†	0.602*	0.658*	0.949	
Income	1.004	1.001	1.006***	1.003†	
Married	0.942	0.694	0.901	0.906	
Any children	0.776	0.761	0.991	0.802	
Retired	0. 839	0.799	1.551*	1.462†	
News consumption profile					
Social media/ in-person	0.840†	0.806*	1.030	0.981	
Print/ broadcast	0.950	0.884	1.041	1.025	
Radio	0.947	0.855†	1.069	1.040	
Online	0.747***	0.703***	0.985	1.139	
Partisanship					
Conservatism		0.942		1.112	
Voted for Trump		0.840		3.508***	
Voted for someone other than Trump or Clinton		1.003		3.373***	
Did not vote		0.127***		0.700	

† $p < 0.10$; * $p < 0.05$; ** $p < 0.01$; *** $p < 0.001$.

Table 3.5

Summary of Associations Between Consumption Profiles and Perceptions of News Reliability

Demographics	Perceptions
Age	N/A
Gender	Men are less likely to think the news is more reliable now and more likely to think it is less reliable.
Race/ethnicity	Black and Hispanic respondents are more likely than white respondents to think the news is more reliable now and less likely to think it is less reliable.
Educational attainment	Those with college degrees are less likely than those without to think the news is more reliable now.
Income	Those with higher incomes are more likely to think the news is less reliable now.
Married	N/A
Retired or working	Retired people are more likely than working people to think the news is less reliable now.
Partisanship	
Political ideology	N/A
Voted in 2016	People who voted for someone other than Clinton are more likely to think the news is less reliable now, and people who voted for anyone (compared with nonvoters) think the news is more reliable now.
News consumption profile	
Social media/in-person	People who rely less on social media/in-person think the news is more reliable now.
Print/broadcast	N/A
Radio	People who rely less on radio think the news is more reliable now.
Online	People who rely less on online news think the news is more reliable now.

NOTE: N/A indicates that variables were not significantly associated with perceptions of news reliability in the multinomial logistic regression.

Although political variables were a relatively minor factor in our analysis of news consumption profiles, they played a significant role in our assessment of perceptions of news reliability. Specifically, when we factored in the political variables (Model 2 in Table 3.4), we found that people who did not vote were less likely than others to report believing that the news is more reliable now than in the past; compared with Clinton voters, those who voted for anyone else were more than three times as likely to report a perception that the news is less reliable than in the past. We found no relationship between perceived reliability and political ideology when voting behavior was also considered.[9] The inclusion of the political variables also affects which sociodemographic characteristics are statistically significant. Nearly all of the demographic factors predicting perceptions of reduced reliability, apart from income and retired status, are absorbed by the political variables, confirming the strong relationship between partisanship and demographic characteristics.[10] News consumption profiles remain relevant, however, with the inclusion of the partisanship variables. Essentially, the more heavily that individuals relied on social media/in-person, radio, or online platforms, the less likely they were to believe that the reliability of the news had changed for the better, although there were no profile links to perceptions of deteriorating reliability.

Which Platforms Are Considered Most Reliable

To further explore media reliability, we asked respondents to report which types of media platforms they found most reliable. Unsurprisingly, perceived reliability differed. Based on our survey, broadcast and cable television were perceived by the most people to be the most reliable, with most people rating one or both in the top two (Figure 3.3). Television is followed by print, online news sites, and radio. Social media and in-person news sources were perceived as the most-reliable sources by the smallest number of respondents.

There are systematic demographic differences in who rated which sources as the most reliable. Comparisons are made with broadcast television because it was most commonly reported as the most reliable platform (26.3 percent of respondents). Tables 3.6 and 3.7 summarize the results: Table 3.6 presents the results of a multinomial logistic model considering the likelihood of rating a platform other than

---

[9] When political ideology was considered without also controlling for the 2016 presidential vote, more-conservative individuals were more likely to report "less reliable."

[10] For a treatment of the relationship between partisanship and demographics, see Liliana Mason, *Uncivil Agreement: How Politics Became Our Identity*, Chicago, Ill.: University of Chicago Press, 2018.

Figure 3.3
Respondents' Top Two Perceived Most-Reliable News Sources

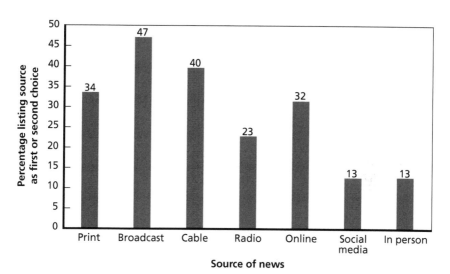

broadcast television as the most reliable platform using demographic, political, and overall perceptions of news reliability; Table 3.7 provides a verbal summary of the relationships.

Demographic and Political Characteristics

Those who viewed print as the most reliable news platform (compared with broadcast television) were significantly more likely to have college degrees and higher incomes, and to be retired and male. Race also matters: Respondents who were black were less likely to list print as the most reliable source of media information. People who voted for candidates other than Trump in 2016 were more likely than those who did vote for Trump to report that print media is the most reliable news platform.

Cable television is significantly distinguished from broadcast television as the more reliable television news platform by those who voted for Trump; compared with those who voted for anyone else, Trump voters were more than twice as likely to report that cable news is more reliable than broadcast news. Conversely, those who voted for Clinton or third-party candidates were less likely to report cable news as the most reliable source of news and might value other sources more

Table 3.6
Perceived Most Reliable News Platform, Compared with Broadcast Television (Relative Risk Ratios)

Characteristic	Print	Cable Television	Radio	Online	Social Media	In-Person
Age	0.990	1.019	0.992	0.969**	1.008	0.992
Male	1.579*	1.438	2.712***	1.944**	0.775	0.933
Black	0.386*	0.988	0.507	0.261*	1.655	1.165
Hispanic	1.199	1.025	0.790	0.589	5.691***	0.619
Other race	1.338	2.007	3.263*	1.392	1.060	0.094*
College	2.224***	0.945	1.161	2.178**	0.541	1.779
Income	1.007***	1.001	1.004	1.000	0.994	0.994
Married	0.706	1.000	0.680	0.965	0.975	2.800*
Any children	0.681	0.963	1.130	1.299	0.855	0.838
Retired	1.700†	1.148	0.569†	1.322	0.313†	0.948
News reliability overall (compared with no change)						
Less reliable now	1.680*	0.961	1.490	1.571	4.253*	4.713***
More reliable now	0.867	2.248**	0.716	1.653	3.342†	2.151
Partisanship						
Conservatism	0.953	0.909	0.933	0.842	1.043	1.075
Voted for Trump	0.296***	2.256**	1.454	1.017	3.337*	1.404
Voted for someone other than Trump or Clinton	1.555	0.940	1.777	4.003***	0.701	5.623**
Did not vote	0.462	1.488	0.549	1.686	4.368*	2.638

† $p < 0.10$; * $p < 0.05$; ** $p < 0.01$; *** $p < 0.001$.

Table 3.7
Summary of Associations Between Consumption Profiles and Most Reliable Platform: Demographic and Political Characteristics

Demographics	Characteristic
Age	Older people are more likely to rate online news as less reliable than broadcast television.
Gender	Men are more likely to rate radio, online, and print news as more reliable than broadcast television.
Race or ethnicity	Black respondents are less likely than white respondents to rate print and online as more reliable than broadcast television; Hispanic respondents are more likely than others to rate social media as the most reliable platform; and those who are not white, Hispanic, or black are more likely to rate radio as the most reliable and least likely to rate in-person as most reliable.
Educational attainment	Those with college degrees are more likely than others to rate print or online news as more reliable than broadcast television.
Income	Those with higher incomes are more likely to rank print news as most reliable.
Married	Married people are more likely than others to rate in-person news as the most reliable.
Retired or working	Retired people are more likely than others to rate print as most reliable, and less likely to rate radio or social media as most reliable.
Partisanship	
Political ideology	N/A
Voted in 2016	Compared with Clinton voters, Trump voters are more likely to rate cable television and social media as more reliable, and print as less reliable. People who voted for someone other than Trump or Clinton are more likely to rate online and in-person as most reliable, and nonvoters rate social media as most reliable.
News reliability overall (compared with no change)	
Less reliable now	People who think the news has become less reliable are more likely to rate print, social media, and in-person as most reliable.
More reliable now	People who think the news has become more reliable are more likely to rate cable television and social media as most reliable.

NOTE: N/A indicates that variables were not significantly associated with ratings of most reliable news platform in the multinomial logistic regression.

highly. No other political or demographic characteristics significantly distinguished those who reported cable television as the most reliable form of news from other respondents.

Radio was more likely to be reported as the most reliable platform by men and by those who identified as something other than white, black, or Hispanic. Retired individuals were less likely than those who were not retired to identify radio as the most reliable platform.

Younger people, men, those who were white (relative to black), and those with college degrees were more likely to report online platforms to be the most reliable (compared with broadcast television). In contrast, Hispanic individuals were substantially more likely than others to list social media as the most reliable news platform. Respondents who voted for anyone other than Trump in 2016 were significantly less likely than Trump voters to list social media as the most reliable news platform.

Finally, obtaining news in person was rated as the most reliable source significantly more by married individuals (nearly three times more than unmarried individuals), and those who voted for someone other than Clinton or Trump (more than five times as likely as Clinton voters). Individuals who identified as something other than white, black, or Hispanic were much less likely than others to list in-person as the most reliable platform.

Perceptions of Overall News Reliability

We also observe links between perceptions of the overall reliability of the news and ratings of the most-reliable news platforms. People who reported believing that the news is less reliable now were more likely to rate print, social media, or in-person news as the most reliable (compared with broadcast television); those who reported believing the news to be more reliable now than in the past were more likely to rate cable television or social media as the most-reliable platforms (compared with broadcast television).

News Consumption Profiles

Although demographic and political characteristics were important in predicting perceived reliability of specific platforms, consumption profiles were also significant, suggesting a clear relationship between the perceived reliability and decisions about consumption (though we cannot say from our analyses which way the arrow moves, from perceived reliability to consumption choices or from consumption choice to perceived reliability. It is likely a mix of both). Table 3.8 presents the expanded multinomial logistic regression results, and Table 3.9 verbally summarizes our analysis. In general, the results suggest that people tend to rate most highly those sources that they use, consistent with prior studies. However, there are some other interesting relationships. For example, those in the radio and online consumption profiles tended to rate almost every other news platform higher than broadcast television news (despite it being the most trusted overall); those in the print and broadcast category were least likely to rate cable television, social media, and online sources of news as the most reliable. We consider these findings in more detail.

Perceived Reliability's Influence on News Consumption Choices

To further explore the relationship between perceived reliability and media use, we compared each respondent's most-used sources with those they rated as the two most reliable. Our analysis indicates that most people (72 percent) get news from sources they believe are among the most reliable. That is, one or both of the platforms they use most frequently are also perceived to be among their top two most-reliable platforms. However, that still leaves 28 percent, almost one-third, of respondents who get most of their news from platforms they have not rated as the most reliable.

Table 3.10 presents results from logistic regressions predicting that individuals use platforms they rate as most reliable, and Table 3.11 presents a verbal summary. There are few demographic and no political characteristics strongly associated with consumption of self-identified reliable sources. There is some evidence that race might matter in whether individuals consume news from sources that they identify as most reliable, but the two models tell slightly different stories about how.[11] Notably, if we do not consider political characteristics, marriage is negatively associated with getting news from a reliable source. In other words, married

---

[11] Again, restricting to only those with partisanship information produces similar results.

Table 3.8
Perceived Most Reliable News Platform, Compared with Broadcast Television, Including News Consumption Profile (Relative Risk Ratios)

Characteristic	Print	Cable Television	Radio	Online	Social Media	In-Person
Age	0.994	1.015	1.001	0.992	1.040†	1.012
Male	1.349	1.112	2.453**	1.682†	0.963	1.063
Black	0.448	1.086	0.578	0.337	2.321	2.000
Hispanic	1.240	0.807	0.688	0.560	7.121***	0.932
Other race	1.242	1.590	3.348*	1.512	1.697	0.109†
College	1.819*	0.837	0.935	1.810†	0.554	1.640
Income	1.007***	1.000	1.004	0.999	0.994	0.997
Married	0.716	0.881	0.736	1.018	1.030	2.792*
Any children	0.651	0.965	1.114	1.154	0.899	0.790
Retired	1.926*	1.198	0.707	1.424	0.330†	1.349
News reliability overall (compared with no change)						
Less reliable now	1.613†	0.966	1.438	1.454	4.132*	5.135***
More reliable now	0.978	1.982*	1.073	2.660*	4.349*	2.234

Table 3.8—Continued

Characteristic	Print	Cable Television	Radio	Online	Social Media	In-Person
News consumption profile						
Social media/in-person	0.869	0.569***	0.823	1.039	2.151*	2.583**
Print/broadcast	1.206	0.433***	0.955	0.725*	0.709†	0.743
Radio	2.019***	1.516**	5.511***	2.084***	0.988	5.611***
Online	1.676***	1.092	1.787***	3.452***	1.778***	0.793
Partisanship						
Conservatism	0.902	0.894	0.934	0.862	1.069	1.044
Voted for Trump	0.381**	2.402**	1.950	1.246	3.752*	1.082
Voted for someone other than Trump or Clinton	1.609	1.049	1.363	4.373***	0.650	4.491**
Did not vote	0.379	1.239	0.278	1.365	5.373*	1.442

† $p < 0.10$; * $p < 0.05$; ** $p < 0.01$; *** $p < 0.001$.

Table 3.9
Summary of Associations Between Consumption Profiles and Perceived Most Reliable Platform

Consumption Profile	Characteristic
Social media/ in-person	People in this profile are more likely to rate social media and in-person as most reliable and cable television as less reliable.
Print/broadcast	People in this profile are more likely to rate cable, online, and social media as less reliable.
Radio	People in this profile are more likely to rate broadcast television and social media as less reliable than print, radio, online, and in-person
Online	People in this profile are more likely to rate broadcast television, cable television, and in-person as less reliable than print, radio, online, and social media.

NOTE: N/A indicates that variables were not significantly associated with rating of most reliable news platform in the multinomial logistic regression.

people are less likely to identify as most reliable those sources that they report using most heavily.

There is also evidence that perceptions of the overall reliability of the news is linked to whether people primarily get their news from reliable platforms; individuals who believe that the news is less reliable now than in the past are *less likely* to get their news via platforms they deem most reliable than either those who perceive no change in the overall reliability of the news or those who believe the news is more reliable now.

The news consumption profile variables are more definitive. Those in the social media/in-person group are less likely to get their news from sources they identify as most reliable (in other words, they rely on social media and other people for news but do not consider these to be the most reliable); those in the print/broadcast profile are more likely to rely on sources they identify as reliable.

Our analysis suggests that although perceived reliability is usually associated with decisions about news consumption, the two are not always related. For example, individuals who believe that overall the news is less reliable now than in the past are about one-third less likely than others to primarily obtain news from platforms they rate

Table 3.10
Primarily Gets News from One of Their Top Two Perceived Most-Reliable Platforms (Odds Ratios; vs. Does Not)

Characteristic	Model 1	Model 2
Age	1.003	1.006
Male	1.268	1.192
Black	0.601†	0.825
Hispanic	0.800	0.720
Other race	0.681	0.428*
College	0.798	0.739
Income	1.000	0.999
Married	0.681*	0.738
Any children	0.826	1.001
Retired	1.158	1.350
News reliability overall (compared with no change)		
Less reliable now	0.735†	0.642*
More reliable now	1.086	1.133
News consumption profile		
Social media/in-person	0.693***	0.753**
Print/broadcast	1.159*	1.141†
Radio	1.022	1.075
Online	0.881	0.947
Partisanship		
Conservatism		0.938
Voted for Trump		1.313
Voted for someone other than Trump or Clinton		1.691
Did not vote		0.936

† $p < 0.10$; * $p < 0.05$; ** $p < 0.01$; *** $p < 0.001$.

Table 3.11
Summary of Variables Linked to an Individual's Likelihood of Getting News from at Least One of Their Two Perceived Most-Reliable Platforms

Demographics	Characteristic
Age	N/A
Gender	N/A
Race/ethnicity	Those who are not white, black, or Hispanic are less likely to get news from platforms they rate as most reliable.
Educational attainment	N/A
Income	N/A
Married	N/A
Retired or working	N/A
Partisanship	
Political ideology	N/A
Voted in 2016	N/A
News reliability overall (compared with no change)	
Less reliable now	Those who report that news is less reliable today than in the past are less likely to get news from platforms they rate as most reliable.
More reliable now	N/A
News consumption profile	
Social media/ in-person	People who rely on social media/in-person more are less likely to get news from platforms they rate as most reliable.
Print/broadcast	People who rely on print/broadcast more are more likely to get news from platforms they rate as most reliable.
Radio	N/A
Online	N/A

NOTE: N/A indicates that variables were not significantly associated with the likelihood of primarily getting news from self-rated reliable platforms in the logistic regression.

as the most reliable. Rather than rely more heavily on news platforms they believe to be the most reliable as a means to mitigate perceived decreases in overall news reliability, these individuals are at greater risk of doing the contrary. Furthermore, as noted, social media/in-person news consumers are less likely to rely primarily on those sources that they rate as most reliable. They do not necessarily view social media or in-person sources as among the most reliable and yet still turn to these sources most often to get news. This suggests that—at least for this group of individuals (typically younger, female, white, and without a college degree)—news consumption might be driven less by perceived reliability of information and more by other factors. We can only speculate on these factors, but literature suggests they might include interest, time, or willingness. As an example, we found that women were more likely to rely on social media and in-person channels but were not more likely to rate these channels as most reliable. One possible explanation (based on previous research on women, their daily demands, and their personal networks) is that women might find it more convenient to be informed about news through social channels (in-person, social media) that are more suited to their larger personal networks,[12] higher levels of communication across those networks,[13] and relative lack of leisure time compared with men.[14] Although this is consistent with the empirical results, it would need to be explored in more depth to directly support any conclusions.

Prior studies that similarly identify a disconnect between credibility and frequency of use among some individuals provide a variety of additional explanations for why people might rely on sources

---

[12] Steve McDonald and Christine A. Mair, "Social Capital Across the Life Course: Age and Gendered Patterns of Network Resources," *Sociological Forum*, Vol. 25, No. 2, June 2010.

[13] Carolyn A. Liebler and Gary D. Sandefur, "Gender Differences in the Exchange of Social Support with Friends, Neighbors, and Co-Workers at Midlife," *Social Science Research*, Vol. 31, No. 3, 2002.

[14] Max Haller, Markus Hadler, and Gerd Kaup, "Leisure Time in Modern Societies: A New Source of Boredom and Stress?" *Social Indicators Research*, Vol. 111, No. 2, 2013.

other than those they identify as the most reliable.[15] Tsfati and Cappella argue that people might get news from sources they believe to be unreliable because, in addition to gathering factual information, news consumption might serve other needs, such as social needs (to stay in touch with other people or society at large) or a need for interesting entertainment.[16] They also argue that the psychological "need for cognition"—the need to think, to understand, to make sense of the world, and to learn about various points of view—motivate consumption regardless of whether the source is perceived as trustworthy.[17] This is another area where additional research would be valuable.

Who Seeks Out Differing Views and How Often

An additional aspect of news consumption behavior we examined was how often individuals sought out sources of news that they knew would offer views that were different from their own. Our inclusion of this question was motivated by recent attention to the negative effects of echo chambers and filter bubbles[18]—and given this attention, it should be noted that this is one case in which respondent answers might be heavily affected by desirability bias because respondents might not want to admit that they do not look for alternative views.[19] Thus, it is possible that respondents will overreport the frequency with which they look for alternative viewpoints; this is an important caveat to keep in mind when assessing these results.

In our survey, one in five respondents (20 percent) reported that they "always or almost always" sought out different views; an additional 54 percent said that they did so "sometimes." Only 17 percent said that they "infrequently" sought out differing sources, and 9 percent said "never or almost never."

---

[15] Fletcher and Park, 2017; Tony Rimmer and David Weaver, "Different Questions, Different Answers? Media Use and Media Credibility," *Journalism Quarterly*, Vol. 64, No. 1, 1987.

[16] Tsfati and Cappella, 2003.

[17] Tsfati and Cappella, 2003.

[18] For example, see Garrett, 2009.

[19] Paul Lavrakas, "Response Bias," *Encyclopedia of Survey Research Methods*, Thousand Oaks, Calif.: Sage, 2008.

Table 3.12 presents the results of a multinomial logistic regression analysis linking how often people reported seeking out news from viewpoints that differ from their own, compared with "sometimes" or "infrequently." A verbal summary of the results is presented in Table 3.13. Married people are particularly less likely to report that they "always or almost always" sought out opposing news sources;[20] black and other race respondents were significantly more likely than others to report "never or almost never." Those with higher education and higher incomes were significantly less likely than others to report they "never or almost never" sought out differing views.

Perceptions of the overall reliability of the news are also linked to whether people seek out alternative viewpoints in the news they consume. People who believe the news to be more reliable now than in the past are more likely to report that they "always or almost always" seek out alternative views, and people who report any change in the overall reliability of the news (either an increase or a decrease in reliability) are less likely to report that they "never or almost never" seek out alternative views than those who think the news is as reliable now as in the past.

Political ideology and vote choice also matter. In terms of seeking out differing views, people who rated their political ideology as more conservative were less likely than more-liberal respondents to report that they "never or almost never" did so; people who reported voting for someone other than Clinton were roughly three times as likely as Clinton voters to report that they "always or almost always" seek out differing views in their news. Those who voted for Trump were three times as likely as non-Trump voters to report "never or almost never." This suggests that Trump voters place themselves in opposite categories of people who either always or never seek out differing views; Clinton voters were much more likely to "sometimes" or "infrequently" seek out differing views than others.

---

[20] Note that this is in opposition to the explanation in Tsfati and Cappella, 2005, of the need for understanding alternative viewpoints as one potential reason for the consumption of news from unreliable sources; married people are less likely to get news from self-identified reliable sources but are also less likely to seek out alternative viewpoints.

Table 3.12
How Often Respondent Seeks Out News with Different Views ("Always
or Almost Always" or "Never or Almost Never" vs. "Sometimes" or
"Infrequently"; Relative Risk Ratios)

Characteristic	Always or Almost Always	Never or Almost Never
Age	0.996	1.005
Male	1.849**	1.206
Black	1.957*	2.958*
Hispanic	0.998	1.451
Other race	1.050	2.872†
College	1.215	0.446*
Income	0.999	0.995†
Married	0.534**	0.899
Any children	1.095	0.947
Retired	0.955	1.023
News reliability overall (compared with no change)		
Less reliable now	1.434	0.271**
More reliable now	1.472†	0.416**
News consumption profile		
Social media/in-person	0.903	1.128
Print/broadcast	1.139	0.844
Radio	1.147	1.022
Online	1.440**	0.732**
Partisanship		
Conservatism	0.946	0.784†
Voted for Trump	2.890***	3.617**
Voted for someone other than Trump or Clinton	3.407***	0.575
Did not vote	1.643	1.160

† $p < 0.10$; * $p < 0.05$; ** $p < 0.01$; *** $p < 0.001$.

Table 3.13
Summary of Characteristics Associated with Likelihood of Seeking Out News with Different Views

Demographics	Characteristic
Age	N/A
Gender	Men are more likely to "always or almost always" seek out differing views.
Race or ethnicity	Black respondents are more likely than white respondents to "always or almost always" or "never or almost never" seek out differing views. Those who are not white, black, or Hispanic are more likely than white respondents to "never or almost never" seek out differing views.
Educational attainment	Those without college degrees are more likely to "never or almost never" seek out differing views.
Income	Those with lower incomes are more likely to "never or almost never" seek out differing views.
Married	Married people are less likely than others to "always or almost always" seek out differing views.
Retired or working	N/A
Partisanship	
Political ideology	More-liberal people are more likely to "never or almost never" seek out differing views.
Voted in 2016	People who voted for Trump are more likely than Clinton voters to "always or almost always" or "never or almost never" seek out differing views. Those who voted for someone other than Trump or Clinton are more likely than Clinton voters to "always or almost always" seek out differing views.
News reliability overall (compared with no change)	
Less reliable now	People who think the news is now less reliable are less likely to "never or almost never" seek out differing views.
More reliable now	People who think the news is now more reliable are more likely to "always or almost always" and less likely to "never or almost never" seek out differing views.
News consumption profile	
Social media/ in-person	N/A
Print/ broadcast	N/A
Radio	N/A
Online	People who rely on online news are more likely to "always or almost always" and less likely to "never or almost never" seek out differing views.

NOTE: N/A indicates that variables were not significantly associated with the likelihood of seeking out news with different viewpoints in the multinomial logistic regression.

Turning to the relationship between likelihood of seeking out alternative viewpoints and news consumption profiles, we found that people who scored highly in the online news consumption profile were significantly more likely to report "always or almost always" seeking out sources of news that offer views different from their own than was the case for other consumer profiles. Online consumers were also significantly less likely to report that they "never or almost never" sought out differing views. It is possible this reflects the ease with which information consumers can seek out diverse viewpoints online, if they choose to do so.

Trust in Institutions and Media Consumption

Limitations

Our analyses have a few limitations worth mentioning. First, we only asked in our survey about news consumption at the level of news platform, not at the level of individual outlets. The quality of news an individual gets through any platform can vary substantially depending on the specific outlets consumed. For example, a consumer who relies on the internet platform for news but is using it to access the websites of leading newspapers will likely receive a very different information diet from someone who uses the internet to access highly polarized editorials or blogs. We hope to expand our work to the outlet level in the future.

Second, we know little about specific frequency of use. We did not ask respondents how frequently or for what duration they typically use the different news platforms, only the rank ordering of use frequency. As noted, a consumer who reads hours of news from newspapers every day will have a very different information diet than a user who reads the newspaper once a month, even if that is still the primary news source for that consumer. Incorporating time use at the outlet level into future iterations of this survey would be valuable.

Third, our analysis applies only to English speakers, as the quarterly ALP Omnibus survey we used to field our questions was not translated into Spanish for Spanish-only respondents. Despite this limitation, our sample was 14 percent Hispanic (unweighted). Future work should seek to explore news consumption habits among Spanish-speaking (and other non-English-speaking) populations in the United States.

Fourth, we interpret the results in terms of non-entertainment news. The survey items referred to "national and international news" and examples of outlets within each platform identified primarily non-entertainment news outlets (e.g., Time or Newsweek magazine, CNN, Breitbart), but we did not explicitly tell respondents to exclude entertainment information consumption. It is possible some respondents included entertainment news in their responses. Consumption behaviors and platform choices related to entertainment versus hard news might differ, and we are unable to further distinguish results.

Finally, our results are dependent on the ways in which our respondents interpret and respond to questions. Social desirability bias, described previously, could affect responses about seeking out other sources of information and about perceived reliability of specific platforms. Individuals might overreport consumption of what they believe to be higher-prestige media (print versus social media, for example). Furthermore, individuals might have an interest in identifying as most reliable those sources that they tend to rely on most often, to maintain internal consistency, even if this response is not entirely truthful. Respondents likely also do not spend a lot of time thinking on a daily basis about how they will assess their degree of trust in media outlets or even ranking their use of different platforms. Their responses on the survey might reflect reactions to the questions without necessarily being indicative of longer-term beliefs and assessments. Overcoming this type of bias is challenging, but in future iterations we might consider using open-ended response questions to get a better sense of why individuals hold the beliefs they do or asking similar related questions at the beginning and end of a longer survey to assess consistency and durability of responses.

CHAPTER FOUR

Discussion

Four Motivating Questions

This study of U.S. news consumers' relationship with the changing U.S. news environment—their preferred news outlets, their sense of the reliability of those and other news outlets, their willingness to seek out news from differing viewpoints, and their demographic and political partisan characteristics connecting them to these aspects of news consumption—was motivated by four interrelated questions:

- How do Americans get their news?
- How are news consumption choices linked to demographic or political characteristics?
- Do news consumers believe the reliability of news has changed, and which news platforms do they believe to be more or less reliable?
- How is the perceived reliability of news associated with news consumption choices?

Overall Findings

Overall, we found that broadcast television, followed by online sources, cable television, and social media are the most-common platforms on which news is consumed by English-speaking U.S. adults.

News Consumption Profiles

From our sample of respondents, we identified four common news consumption profiles (described and differentiated by people's relative level of use of four different packages to obtain news): print and broadcast television platforms, online platforms, radio, and social media and in-person sources. An individual's use of various sources of news is represented by how highly he or she scores on each of these four profiles.

These news consumption profiles are useful for several reasons. Most importantly, they provide a more holistic picture of news consumers, allowing us to identify which types of sources are often used together and the specific demographic characteristics associated with specific patterns of media consumption. They also allow us to explore how news consumption fits in with other political and social behaviors, offering a more nuanced view of how news consumption might fit into individual lives. For example, working individuals tend to score higher on radio sources (possibly while commuting to work). Married individuals are less likely to rely on print or broadcast news, more likely to perceive in-person communication as the most reliable method of obtaining news, and less likely to report seeking out news that offers different viewpoints (possibly because of time constraints). As noted elsewhere, however, we will also need information on specific sources used and duration of use to fully assess information consumption habits. Collecting and analyzing this information will be an important next step in this line of research.

Perceived Reliability of News Platforms

Two variables, age and political attitudes and behavior, appear to be the most-salient predictors of news consumption decisions and perceived reliability of information sources. With respect to age, as discussed in earlier chapters, younger users are more likely to lean on online and in-person information channels; older users are more likely to get news through more-traditional means—broadcast or cable news and print media. Across users of all ages, however, social media and in-person communication sources are least likely to be perceived as reliable sources of news, even by those who rely primarily on them. Broadcast and cable television were viewed as the most reliable, followed by print and online sources. Tables 4.1 through 4.3 summarize these and the other overall findings we outline later; Table 4.1 presents results in terms of characteristics and behaviors associated with each news consumption profile factor; Table 4.2 summarizes results related to perceptions of overall reliability of the news; and Table 4.3 summarizes results related to our political measures.

Partisanship and voting behavior are relevant to news consumption choices and perceptions of reliability. People who reported holding a more conservative political ideology were less likely to score highly

Table 4.1
Summary of Relationships Between News Consumption Profiles and Other Characteristics and Behaviors

Characteristic	Social Media/ In-Person	Print/ Broadcast	Radio	Online
Age	Younger	N/A	N/A	Younger
Gender	Female	N/A	Male	Male
Race or ethnicity	White	Non-Hispanic	N/A	Not black
Educational attainment	No college degree	N/A	College degree	College degree
Income	Lower income	N/A	N/A	Higher income
Married	N/A	Not married	N/A	N/A
Retired or working	N/A	N/A	Working	N/A
Partisanship				
Political ideology	N/A	N/A	N/A	More liberal
Vote choice in 2016	More likely to have voted for someone other than Clinton or Trump	More likely to have voted for Clinton	N/A	More likely to have voted for Clinton
Perception of change in news reliability	Does not think news is more reliable now	N/A	N/A	Does not think news is more reliable now
Consumption behaviors				
Uses reliable platforms	No	Yes	N/A	N/A
Seeks out differing views	N/A	N/A	N/A	Yes

NOTE: N/A indicates that variables were not significantly associated with the news consumption profile factors in the regressions.

Table 4.2
Summary of Relationships Between Perceptions of Overall News Reliability
and Other Characteristics and Behaviors

Characteristics of People Who Think the News Is . . .	. . . More Reliable Now	. . . Less Reliable Now
Race or ethnicity	Black and Hispanic	N/A
Educational attainment	Less than a college degree	N/A
Income	N/A	Higher income
Retired or working	N/A	Retired
Partisanship		
Political ideology	N/A	N/A
Voted in 2016	Voted (vs. did not vote)	Voted for someone other than Clinton
News consumption profile		
Social media/in-person	Use social media/in-person less	N/A
Print/broadcast	N/A	N/A
Radio	Use radio less	N/A
Online	Use online news less	N/A
Consumption behaviors		
Uses reliable platforms	N/A	Less likely to use self-rated reliable platforms
Seeks out differing views	Always or almost always	Less likely than people who do not think the reliability of the news has changed to say never or almost never

NOTE: N/A indicates that variables were not significantly associated with perceptions of the reliability of the news in the regressions.

on the online consumption and less likely to report "never or almost never" seeking out alternative views in their news. More-liberal individuals, conversely, tended to score higher on the online consumption profile and were more likely to report "never or almost never" seeking out alternative views than more-conservative respondents.

Compared with people who reported voting for Clinton in 2016, people who reported voting for Trump scored lower on the print/broadcast television profile. Trump voters were also more likely to believe that the news is less reliable now than in the past and to rate cable tele-

Table 4.3
Summary of Results Related to Political Partisanship

	Self-Rated Political Ideology	Voted for Trump (vs. Clinton)	Voted for Someone Other Than Trump or Clinton	Did Not Vote
Platforms used	More conservative ideology associated with lower likelihood of getting news from online platforms	Less likely to get news from print/broadcast or online platforms	More likely to get news from social media/in-person platforms	N/A
Overall perception of news reliability	N/A	More likely to believe the news is less reliable now	More likely to believe the news is less reliable now	Less likely to think the news is more reliable now
More-reliable platforms	N/A	More likely to report the most-reliable news platforms are cable television and social media Less likely to report that print is the most reliable news platform	More likely to report the most-reliable news platforms are online and in person	More likely to report the most reliable news platform is social media
Gets news from reliable platforms	N/A	N/A	N/A	N/A
Seeks out differing views	More-conservative ideology associated with lower likelihood of "never or almost never" seeking out differing views	More likely to "always or almost always" or "never or almost never" seek out news with differing viewpoints	More likely to "always or almost always" seek out news with differing viewpoints	N/A

NOTE: N/A indicates that variables were not significantly associated with the news consumption profile factors in the regressions.

vision and social media as the most-reliable platforms, and they were less likely to rate print as reliable. Compared with those who voted for Clinton, those who voted for someone other than Trump or Clinton were more likely to get news from social media/in-person, more likely to believe the news is less reliable now than in the past, and more likely to rate online and in-person platforms as most reliable. Taken together, this suggests that those who voted for Clinton are less skeptical of more-traditional news delivery platforms; they also tend to favor print as their source for news, are much less likely to believe that the reliability of news has declined over time, and less likely to rate online or especially in-person news sources as the most-reliable platforms. Those who voted for Clinton were also less likely than other voters to report that they "always or almost always" seek out news sources that offer views different from their own, in addition to the effect associated with liberal ideology.

Factors Associated with News Consumption

Political Ideology and Behavior

The analyses presented in this report focus on demographic and political factors linked to news consumption and find that both are associated with media use profiles and attitudes toward the platforms that compose those profiles. Specifically, our results indicate that political ideology and behavior are tied to news consumption—although political behavior (voter turnout and choice) seems to be a stronger predictor than partisanship. Self-rated political ideology and voting behavior in the 2016 presidential election were each tied to different aspects of news consumption and beliefs, but 2016 voting behavior appeared to have a more substantively significant effect than partisanship and to affect many more aspects of news consumption.

People who rated themselves as more conservative on the political ideology scale scored significantly lower on the online dimension of news consumption profiles than did more-liberal individuals, and they were less likely to report that they "never or almost never" sought out alternative viewpoints from the news. Those who self-identified as more liberal tended to score higher on the online consumption profile and were more likely to report "never or almost never" seeking out alternative views than more conservative respondents.

Voting behavior, in contrast, was associated with more aspects of news consumption and beliefs than were underlying political ideologies. Our analyses report results relative to Clinton voters because they were the largest category. First, people who reported voting for someone other than Clinton in 2016 were significantly (more than three times) more likely than others to report a belief that the news is less reliable now than in the past. Those who voted for third-party candidates were more likely to rate online and in-person platforms as the most reliable (four times more likely than Clinton voters) and to score higher on the social media/in-person profile.

Trump voters were more likely than other voters to rate cable television (two times) or social media (three and a half times) as the most-reliable news platforms and significantly less likely to rate print as the most reliable. They scored significantly lower than Clinton voters on the print/broadcast dimension of news consumption profiles, and were (three times) more likely than voters for any other candidate to report either extreme (always or never) with regard to whether they sought out news with alternative views to their own. Recall that a higher level of self-identified conservative ideology was negatively associated with reporting "never or almost never" seeking out news from differing viewpoints.

Taken together, this suggests that those who voted for Clinton rather than someone else were less skeptical of more-traditional news delivery platforms; they tended to favor print as their source for news, were much less likely to believe that the reliability of news has declined over time, and were also less likely to rate online or especially in-person news as the most-reliable platforms. Those who voted for Clinton were also less likely than other voters to report that they "always or almost always" seek out news sources that offer views different from their own. Furthermore, those who did not vote in the 2016 presidential election were even less likely than others to believe that the reliability of news had improved over time, and, similar to Trump voters, were more likely to rate social media as the most reliable news platform.

Demographics

It would be a mistake to suggest that individuals' news consumption profiles and their attitudes toward news reliability were influenced only by political ideology or engagement, however.[1] Instead, our results underscored the importance of demographic factors—such as age, education, and marital status.

Age. Age was shown to be an important predictor of news consumption profile but of relatively little else. Younger individuals were more likely to fit the social media/in-person and online consumption profiles; older individuals were more likely to fit the print/broadcast television profile. As previously noted, older individuals are more likely to get news using more-traditional platforms than are younger people, who are more likely to get news from social media/in-person or online.

Education. We observed educational differences in nearly every topic we examined. Those with college educations were less likely to report a heavy reliance on social media/in-person news compared with radio and online sources. They were also less likely to think that the reliability of the news had changed—for better or for worse—compared with the past. College-educated individuals were more likely to rate print and online platforms as being most reliable and were less likely than those with lower levels of educational attainment to report "never or almost never" seeking out news from alternative viewpoints.

Marital status. One demographic characteristic that appeared several times in our analyses was the connection between marriage and news consumption behaviors. Married people scored marginally lower on their reliance on print/broadcast and were nearly three times as likely as nonmarried individuals to rate in-person as the most reliable platform for news. Married people were also roughly one-half as likely as others to report that they "always or almost always" sought out sources with differing views. One possible explanation is that individuals cannot easily consume print media at the same time as other

---

[1] Although political ideology and voting behavior were assessed several years before news consumption habits, it is also possible that news consumption habits influence political ideology and voting behaviors. To assess causal direction, we would require data tracking changes in both over time.

activities (such as housework) but can consume other platforms, such as radio or in-person communication.

The prevailing theoretical framework for understanding the relationship between marriage and community life is that marriage is a "greedy institution," in that intense couple relationships come at the expense of other connections and are particularly demanding of women's time through housework.[2] Married women, but not men, are also significantly less likely to volunteer after marriage and volunteer fewer hours.[3]

Obtaining news from platforms that respondents themselves have rated as more reliable, or that offer a variety of viewpoints, might be a similar premium that married people are less able to enjoy. This interpretation is further strengthened by the finding that married people who relied more heavily on social media/in-person platforms were especially less likely to report getting news from platforms they viewed as most reliable. At the same time, married people are significantly more likely to vote in elections than unmarried people;[4] those who might encounter challenges to obtaining news and information from platforms they deem most reliable, therefore, might also be among the ones most engaged in political activity.

Implications for Truth Decay

These results have implications for how we might respond to *Truth Decay*—the diminishing reliance on facts, data, and analysis in American public life—and its relationship to media and news consumption. Our analyses suggest that news consumption choices might be influ-

---

[2] Naomi Gerstel and Natalia Sarkisian, "Marriage: The Good, the Bad, and the Greedy," *Contexts*, Vol. 5, No. 4, 2006; and Natalia Sarkisian and Naomi Gerstel, "Till Marriage Do Us Part: Adult Children's Relationships with Their Parents," *Journal of Marriage and Family*, Vol. 70, No. 2, 2008.

[3] Christopher J. Einolf and Deborah Philbrick, "Generous or Greedy Marriage? A Longitudinal Study of Volunteering and Charitable Giving," *Journal of Marriage and Family*, Vol. 76, No. 3, 2014.

[4] Jan E. Leighley and Jonathan Nagler, *Who Votes Now? Demographics, Issues, Inequality, and Turnout in the United States*, Princeton, N.J.: Princeton University Press, 2013.

enced not only by political beliefs but also by demographics, respon-sibilities, and time demands or constraints. If this is true, then just improving the quality of information available or providing individuals skills to understand and evaluate media sources more effectively might not be sufficient to address Truth Decay. Instead, doing so might require changing people's attitudes toward consuming news (reinforc-ing its importance and clarifying its benefits) and offering new ways to access reliable news that are as easy as social media and in-person com-munication. What those new platforms or mechanisms might look like should be an area for future research.

More broadly, this report's analyses present three key implications relevant to the overall Truth Decay agenda, a part of which is focused on understanding how people use and relate with news.

Consumption Choices and Social Media

Much attention has been paid to the increasing reliance of news con-sumers on social media as a source of news because of the ease with which misinformation and disinformation spreads through that plat-form and because of perceptions that the quality of its information and discourse is lower than that on other platforms.[5] We do not evalu-ate these arguments in this report, but we can offer some insight into trends in the use of social media for news.

According to our analysis, 30 percent of respondents reported relying on social media as their primary or secondary source of news, ranking it somewhere in the middle in terms of use compared with other sources. However, there is evidence in our data that even those 30 percent of consumers who do rely heavily on social media for news are likely also using other sources of news. This is consistent with past work discussed at the beginning of this report focused on media com-plementarity and the way that different sources might function together to meet an individual's information needs.[6] Continuing to track how

---

[5] Hunt Alcott, Matthew Gentzkow, and Chuan Yu, *Trends in the Diffusion of Misinformation on Social Media*, Cambridge, Mass.: National Bureau of Economic Research, NBER Working Paper No. 25500, 2018; and Rande Price, "Oxford Research Documents the Alarming Rise of Disinformation on Social Media," *Digital Content Next*, September 21, 2018.

[6] See for example, Van Damme et al., 2015.

people use social media—and especially which specific sources they rely on—will be an important area for future research.

These findings are relevant to a recent study by Grinberg and colleagues that estimated that exposure to fake news on Twitter during the 2016 U.S. presidential election was rare, but that engagement with fake news sources was extremely concentrated: 1 percent of individuals accounted for 80 percent of fake news exposures, and 0.1 percent accounted for nearly 80 percent of fake news sources shared.[7] Likelihood of engaging with fake news sources on Twitter increased substantially for older people and exponentially for political conservatives. Our results show that those who voted for Trump are much more likely to rate social media as the most reliable platform, but conservatives in general are more likely to think that the news is less reliable now. Thus, one interpretation of their overall perception of reduced news reliability is that it might be a response to greater exposure to fake news. However, their likelihood of using social media platforms is not different from more-liberal respondents, and younger people overall were more likely to rely on social media platforms, which raises questions about whether there are further differences among individuals in their news-accessing and news-sharing behaviors on social media. We plan to examine this question in future research.

News Consumption and Demographics

Our results indicate that people obtain news in different ways—relying on different types of sources and with varying degrees of trust in the news overall and in specific news delivery platforms. Partisanship explains some of these differences but certainly not all of them. Such factors as vote choice, propensity to vote, age, gender, education, and marital status all play a significant role in explaining news consumption. Different news consumption profiles are associated with different personal and demographic attributes and living situations and so might also reflect an individual's access to information in terms of time, technology, and availability.

---

[7] Nir Grinberg, Kenneth Joseph, Lisa Friedland, Briony-Swire-Thompson, and David Lazer, "Fake News on Twitter During the 2016 U.S. Presidential Election," *Science*, Vol. 363, No. 6425, 2019.

The results in this report consider choices between platforms, not specific news outlets, but these insights still have broad implications for efforts aimed at improving how people access, interpret, and evaluate news. Although much attention has been paid to media literacy education as a necessity in the information environment, the analysis here suggests that perceptions of reliability and issues surrounding ease of access to reliable news might be equally important.

Media Reliability

Finally, this study considered perceptions of media reliability and trust in the media. Our analysis confirmed that many people are skeptical of the reliability of news overall but that a small minority thinks that reliability is increasing. This underscores the importance of considering disaggregated data when studying media consumption and trust in the media.

Perceptions of the overall reliability of the news are linked to whether people seek out alternative viewpoints in the news they consume. People who believe the news to be more reliable now than in the past are more likely to report that they "always or almost always" seek out alternative views in the news, and people who report any change in the overall reliability of the news (either an increase or a decrease in reliability) are less likely than those who think the news is as reliable now as in the past to report that they "never or almost never" seek out alternative views. Furthermore, individuals who say that the news is less reliable now than in the past are about one-third less likely than others to primarily obtain news from platforms they rate as the most reliable. Rather than rely more heavily on news platforms they believe to be the most reliable as a means to mitigate perceived decreases in overall news reliability, these individuals are at greater risk of doing the contrary.

Attitudes also vary about the reliability of different types of news platforms. Broadcast and cable news are considered the most-reliable sources, followed by print and online sources, which in turn are followed by social media and in-person communication. Our analysis also shows that attitudes toward the media (whether measured as reliability or trust) are linked to consumption. For most users, perceived reliability matters. News media consumers tend to rely most heavily on those sources that they perceive as most reliable, though, as we have noted, there are some exceptions, such as those who rely on other people and social media for news, some married people, and (perhaps surprisingly) those who believe the news is less reliable overall. Clearly the belief that news is less reliable now than in the past is not sufficient to motivate many people to seek out news that they do believe comes from reliable platforms—in fact, our findings are the opposite.

Prior studies have tended to use the terms *trust* and *credibility* interchangeably; our use of the word *reliability* was intended to assess the degree to which respondents felt that they could rely or consistently depend on a given news platform to provide accurate information. Nonetheless, we were able to show that direct assessment of "trust" in various news platforms mapped strongly onto the reliability-based results, indicating a close similarity to the literature on media trust.

Much attention has been paid to the declining trust in media organizations and the effect of that decline on the ability of the media to serve in its role as provider of information and on the willingness of individuals to engage seriously with news.[8] The results here, however, remind us that factors related to both supply and demand could improve the trust that individuals have in the media. For some consumers, trust and consumption appear to be closely linked, so that levels of trust in media might drive consumption choices, and consumption choices, in turn, might feed back into trust. For others, trust might not be as closely linked to consumption but might be shaped by environmental or individual characteristics. Future work examining this potential feedback loop over time is warranted. For all consumers, choices about media consumption are likely linked to individual characteristics, preferences, and behaviors. As a result, attempts to alter or improve the relationship between media outlets and consumers are likely to require attention not only to the supply side of the information ecosystem but also to the demand side and the ways in which people access news. Future work that explores news consumption in this more holistic way will be important as the informational ecosystem grows increasingly diverse and complex.

---

[8] For example, see Chris Peters and Marcel Jeroen Broersma, eds., *Rethinking Journalism: Trust and Participation in a Transformed News Landscape*, New York: Routledge, 2013.

Ranked Data Factor Analysis Procedure

This appendix describes the factor analysis procedure that was used to identify the news consumption profiles.

Method

We used EFA to analyze the platforms that people use to receive news, focusing on print, broadcast, cable, radio, online, social media, or in-person communication.

The participants were asked to rank the top four out of the seven media sources. We coded the top four as 1–4, with 4 being the highest rank. We treated the rest of the unranked sources (i.e., missing responses) as rank 0.

We then proceeded with a monotonic transformation of ranked sources via the PROC PRINQUAL procedure followed by EFA in SAS. Our initial principal components analysis suggests four principal components. Using that as a guideline, the PROC PRINQUAL procedure transforms each variable to be as much as possible like the first principal component (or, more generally, to be close to the space defined by the first $N = 4$ principal components). Before PRINQUAL, four components account for 70 percent of the variance of the untransformed ranked data. After the monotonic transformation, more than 99 percent of the variance of the transformed data were explained by the four extracted factors (see Figure A.1).

With the transformed responses, we proceed with EFA to investigate types of communication using the VARIMAX orthogonal rotation. Eigenvalues,[1] scree plot,[2] and proportion of variance explained were used to guide decisions about the number of factors to extract from seven sources of information. Based on the rotated factor loading pattern, we examined the interpretability of EFA results. When the criteria of the number of factors extracted were satisfied and the results were interpretable, we proceeded to scoring, using the coefficients generated from EFA results.

Results

EFA results indicated a four-factor solution based on an overall evaluation of eigenvalues, scree plot, and variance explained. Kaiser's criterion considers factors with an eigenvalue greater than 1 as common factors. As is shown in the scree plot (see Figure A.1), four eigenvalues are above 1 and the biggest drop in eigenvalues is between #4 and #5, suggest-

Figure A.1
Scree Plot and Variance Explained by Factor Analysis, Suggesting Four Factors Should Be Retained

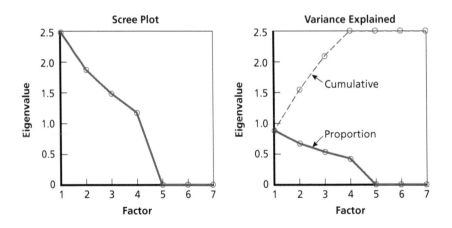

[1]   Henry F. Kaiser, "The Application of Electronic Computers for Factor Analysis," *Educational and Psychological Measurement*, Vol. 20, No. 1, 1960.

[2]   Raymond B. Cattell, "The Scree Test for the Number of Factors," *Multivariate Behavioral Research*, Vol. 1, No. 2, 1966.

ing four factors be kept. The loading patterns (see Table A.1) suggest four primary ways in which people received information: (1) Social media and in-person communication were highly ranked; (2) print and broadcast television were highly ranked; (3) online was highly ranked; and (4) radio was highly ranked. Scoring coefficients (also shown in Table A.1) are used to generate factor scores for each person on each of these four dimensions. Scores on each factor have a mean of 0 and a standard deviation of 1.

Table A.1
EFA Estimated Loadings and Scoring Coefficients

	Factor 1	Factor 2	Factor 3	Factor 4
EFA estimated factor loadings				
Print	−0.02	0.98	0.02	0.20
Broadcast	0.00	0.83	0.00	−0.55
Cable	−0.57	−0.43	−0.69	−0.09
Radio	−0.02	0.02	0.02	1.00
Online	−0.18	−0.09	0.98	0.00
Social media	1.00	−0.02	−0.04	−0.02
In person	1.00	−0.02	−0.04	−0.02
Scoring coefficients				
Print	−0.08	0.68	−0.13	1.02
Broadcast	−0.02	0.29	0.02	−1.38
Cable	−0.23	−0.19	−0.41	−0.28
Radio	0.00	0.00	0.00	0.00
Online	−0.12	−0.15	0.73	−0.23
Social media	0.85	−0.12	−0.11	−0.18
In person	0.00	0.00	0.00	0.00

Study Descriptive Statistics

Table B.1 lists the unweighted statistics for the variables used in this report.

Table B.1
Study Variable Descriptive Statistics (Unweighted)

Variable	Mean or Proportion	Standard Deviation
Age	56.66	14.30
Sex		
Male	0.44	0.50
Female (reference)	0.56	
Race/ethnicity		
Non-Hispanic black	0.10	0.29
Hispanic	0.14	0.35
Other race	0.05	0.22
Non-Hispanic white (reference)	0.71	0.45
Has a college degree (yes)	0.23	0.42
Household income (in thousands)	76.17	60.40
Married (yes)	0.58	0.49
Any children in the household (yes)	0.47	0.50
Retired (yes)	0.32	0.46
Do you find the news you currently receive . . .		
. . . Less reliable than in the past	0.41	0.49
. . . More reliable than in the past	0.15	0.36
. . . About the same (reference)	0.44	
News consumption profile factors		
Social media/in-person	0.00	1.00
Print/broadcast	0.00	1.00
Radio	0.00	1.00
Online	0.00	1.00
Partisanship		
Conservatism		
"How would you describe your political viewpoints?" (on a scale from 1 = very liberal to 5 = very conservative)	2.96	1.16
Voted for Trump	0.36	0.48
Voted for someone other than Trump or Clinton	0.08	0.27
Did not vote	0.09	0.29
Voted Clinton (reference)	0.47	0.50

Trust in Institutions and News Consumption

As a supplement to our analysis of how perceived reliability shapes news consumption, we explored the link between perceived *reliability* of news platforms and explicit *trust* in particular news platforms to further validate our reliability measure. We also measured the links between *trust* and news consumption profiles. To explore how trust affects news consumption, we linked the data for our 2018 survey with data on institutional trust collected from a separate survey of 1,009 ALP respondents conducted in April 2018 by matching the data for common participants. The survey contained attitudes toward national and local newspapers, cable and broadcast television, and social media, ranging from complete distrust to complete trust.[1]

We then conducted a multinomial regression using reported trust in news platforms (from April 2018) as an explanatory variable and perceived reliability as the dependent variable. In short, the results are similar to the previous results in Table 3.6 but factor in the trust measures as additional covariates. We find that reported trust and perceived reliability are closely correlated. Trust in national newspapers is strongly predictive of rating print as the most reliable news platform; trust in cable news is similarly linked to rating cable television as the most reliable platform; trust in broadcast news is significantly linked with rating broadcast television as more reliable than cable television, radio, or online news platforms. Finally, trust in social media was sig-

---

[1]   All respondents in the institutional trust survey were participants in the larger media reliability survey. We were able to match 38 percent of the responses in the original data set using the new data.

nificantly linked to rating social media as the more reliable platform and to rating cable television and print as more reliable than broadcast television. Thus, our results suggest that, conceptually, trust and reliability are closely related for consumers when assessing various news platforms.

The measures of trust similarly predicted the use patterns identified in the media consumption profiles. Specifically, trust in social media is associated with a higher likelihood of being in the social media/in-person group (so, those who report higher trust in social media are more likely to use social media and in-person news sources most often). Trust in national newspapers was positively associated with being in the print/broadcast group. Trust in cable news is negatively associated with being in the social media/in-person, print/broadcast, and online consumption profiles, and trust in broadcast news is negatively associated with the likelihood of being in the radio consumption profile. These results suggest that just as perceived reliability is associated with news consumption choices, a respondent's trust in various news platforms is also associated with information use habits.

Table C.1 reports the results of a multinomial regression using reported trust in news platforms (from April 2018) as an explanatory variable and perceived reliability as the dependent variable. The results in Table C.1 are similar to those in Table 3.6 but factor in the trust measures as additional covariates.

Table C.2 is similar to the OLS regressions linking characteristics to news consumption profiles in Table 3.1 but add in the trust measures as further controls.

Table C.1
Most Reliable News Platform, Compared with Broadcast Television,
Including Trust Measures (Relative Risk Ratios)

Characteristics	Print	Cable Television	Radio	Online	Social Media	In-Person
Age	0.993	1.003	0.976	0.967*	0.952†	0.984
Male	2.005*	1.298	3.593**	2.487*	0.380	1.359
Black	0.167*	0.425	0.100*	0.516	0.000***	0.174
Hispanic	1.378	1.005	0.051***	0.742	0.725	1.062
Other race	1.248	1.423	6.998*	3.600	6.113	0.000***
College	1.258	0.700	0.555	1.849	6.343	4.017*
Income	1.007*	0.998	1.005	0.996	0.969*	0.975**
Married	0.993	1.213	0.803	1.829	0.670	2.599
Any children	0.386**	1.008	1.086	0.772	0.483	1.361
Retired	1.418	1.645	1.090	2.025	6.134†	2.193
Conservatism	0.934	0.724†	0.716	0.768	3.492**	1.006
Voted for Trump	0.458	0.969	1.151	2.339	1.346	0.421
Voted for someone other than Trump or Clinton	1.615	0.780	1.600	9.336***	2.581	1.440
Did not vote	0.098*	0.367†	0.266	1.003	7.186†	0.273
Trust in national newspapers	1.238*	0.741**	1.024	1.356*	0.745	0.695**
Trust in local newspapers	0.996	0.923	1.011	0.897	0.783	0.937
Trust in cable news	0.934	1.517***	1.084	1.053	0.780	0.954
Trust in broadcast news	0.862	0.809*	0.760*	0.645**	1.150	1.009
Trust in social media	1.092	1.147†	0.878	1.090	2.546***	1.064

NOTE: For this analysis, $N = 1,008$. † $p < 0.10$; * $p < 0.05$; ** $p < 0.01$; *** $p < 0.001$.

Table C.2
Characteristics Associated with News Consumption Profile Factors, Including Trust Measures (OLS Coefficients)

	Social Media/ In-Person	Print/ Broadcast	Radio	Online
Age	−0.016***	0.008†	−0.005	−0.014**
Male	−0.240**	−0.060	0.115	0.070
Black	−0.065	0.331*	0.039	−0.239
Hispanic	−0.200	−0.199	−0.423*	−0.131
Other race	−0.474	0.022	0.053	0.564
College	−0.073	0.063	0.141†	0.093
Income	−0.002*	0.000	0.000	0.001
Married	−0.205*	−0.020	0.017	0.015
Any children	0.126	−0.151	−0.030	0.025
Retired	−0.052	−0.129	−0.171	0.102
Conservatism	−0.027	0.088	−0.017	−0.008
Voted for Trump	0.215	0.046	0.031	−0.295†
Voted for someone other than Trump or Clinton	0.535**	−0.373	−0.070	0.074
Did not vote	0.105	−0.025	−0.032	−0.110
Trust in national newspapers	0.014	0.099***	0.041	−0.006
Trust in local newspapers	−0.005	−0.031	−0.031	0.006
Trust in cable news	−0.090**	−0.045†	0.005	−0.050†
Trust in broadcast news	0.036	0.026	−0.090*	0.002
Trust in social media	0.052*	−0.041	−0.010	−0.004

NOTE: For this analysis, $N = 1,008$. † $p < 0.10$; * $p < 0.05$; ** $p < 0.01$; *** $p < 0.001$.

References

Ahlers, Douglas, "News Consumption and the New Electronic Media," *Harvard International Journal of Press/Politics*, Vol. 11, No. 1, 2006, pp. 29–52.

Alcott, Hunt, Matthew Gentzkow, and Chuan Yu, *Trends in the Diffusion of Misinformation on Social Media*, Cambridge, Mass.: National Bureau of Economic Research, NBER Working Paper No. 25500, 2018.

Althaus, Scott, Anne M. Cizmar, and James G. Gimpel, "Media Supply, Audience Demand, and the Geography of News Consumption in the United States," *Political Communication*, Vol. 26, No. 3, 2009, pp. 249–277.

Baldwin, Thomas F., and Marianne Barrett, "Uses and Values for News on Cable Television," *Journal of Broadcasting and Electronic Media*, Vol. 36, No. 2, 1992, pp. 225–234.

Barthel, Michael, "Newspapers Fact Sheet," webpage, Pew Research Center, June 13, 2018. As of August 4, 2018:
http://www.journalism.org/fact-sheet/newspapers/

Bennet, Stephen Earl, Staci L. Rhine, and Richard S. Flickinger, "Assessing Americans' Opinions About the News Media's Fairness in 1996 and 1998," *Political Communication*, Vol. 18, No. 2, 2001, pp. 163–182.

Bennett, Stephen Earl, Staci L. Rhine, Richard S. Flickinger, and Linda L. M. Bennett, "'Video Malaise' Revisited: Public Trust in the Media and Government," *Harvard International Journal of Press/Politics*, Vol. 4, No. 4, 1999, pp. 8–23.

Blumler, Jay G., and Elihu Katz, *The Uses of Mass Communications*, Beverly Hills, Calif.: Sage Publications, 1974.

Bogart, Leo, "The Public's Use and Perception of Newspapers," *Public Opinion Quarterly*, Vol. 48, No. 4, January 1, 1984, pp. 709–719.

Bucy, Erik P., "Media Credibility Reconsidered: Synergy Effects Between On-Air and Online News," *Journalism and Mass Communication Quarterly*, Vol. 80, No. 2, 2003, pp. 247–264.

Carman, Katherine, "Well Being 496: Trust in Government," RAND American Life Panel, webpage, April 2018. As of September 5, 2019: https://alpdata.rand.org/index.php?page=data&p=showsurvey&syid=496

Carter, Richard F., and Bradley S. Greenberg, "Newspaper or Television: Which Do You Believe?" *Journalism Quarterly*, Vol. 42, No. 1, 1965, pp. 29–34.

Cattell, Raymond B., "The Scree Test for the Number of Factors," *Multivariate Behavioral Research*, Vol. 1, No. 2, 1966, pp. 245–276.

Chan, Joey Ka-Ching, and Louis Leung, "Lifestyles, Reliance on Traditional News Media and Online News Adoption," *New Media & Society*, Vol. 7, No. 3, 2005, pp. 357–382.

Coffey, Steve, and Horst Stipp, "The Interactions Between Computer and Television Usage," *Journal of Advertising Research*, Vol. 37, No. 2, 1997, pp. 61–68.

Dutta-Bergman, Mohan J., "Complementarity in Consumption of News Types Across Traditional and New Media," *Journal of Broadcasting & Electronic Media*, Vol. 48, No. 1, 2004, pp. 41–60.

Einolf, Christopher J., and Deborah Philbrick, "Generous or Greedy Marriage? A Longitudinal Study of Volunteering and Charitable Giving," *Journal of Marriage and Family*, Vol. 76, No. 3, 2014, pp. 573–586.

Faber, Ronald J., Stephen D. Reese, and Leslie H. Steeves, "Spending Time with the News Media: The Relationship Between Reliance and Use," *Journal of Broadcasting and Electronic Media*, Vol. 29, No. 4, 1985, pp. 445–450.

Fischer, Sara, "92% of Republicans Think Media Intentionally Reports Fake News," Axios, June 27, 2018. As of August 4, 2018: https://www.axios.com/trump-effect-92-percent-republicans-media-fake-news-9c1bbf70-0054-41dd-b506-0869bb10f08c.html

Flanagin, Andrew J., and Miriam J. Metzger, "Internet Use in the Contemporary Media Environment," *Human Communication Research*, Vol. 27, No. 1, 2001, pp. 153–181.

Fletcher, Richard, and Sora Park, "The Impact of Trust in the News Media on Online News Consumption and Participation," *Digital Journalism*, Vol. 5, No. 10, 2017, pp. 1281–1299.

Garrett, R. Kelly, "Echo Chambers Online? Politically Motivated Selective Exposure Among Internet News Users," *Journal of Computer-Mediated Communication*, Vol. 14, No. 2, 2009, pp. 265–285.

Garrett, R. Kelly, and Natalie Jomini Stroud, "Partisan Paths to Exposure Diversity: Differences in Pro- and Counterattitudinal News Consumption," *Journal of Communication*, Vol. 64, No. 4, 2014, pp. 680–701.

Gaskins, Benjamin, and Jennifer Jerit, "Internet News: Is It a Replacement for Traditional Media Outlets?" *International Journal of Press/Politics*, Vol. 17, No. 2, 2012, pp 190–213.

Gaziano, Cecilie, and Kristin McGrath, "Measuring the Concept of Credibility," *Journalism Quarterly*, Vol. 63, No. 3, 1986, pp. 451–462.

Gentzkow, Matthew, "Valuing New Goods in a Model with Complementarity: Online Newspapers," *American Economic Review*, Vol. 97, No. 3, 2007, pp. 713–744.

Gerstel, Naomi, and Natalia Sarkisian, "Marriage: The Good, the Bad, and the Greedy," *Contexts*, Vol. 5, No. 4, 2006, pp. 16–21.

Glynn, Carroll J., Michael E. Huge, and Lindsay H. Hoffman, "All the News That's Fit to Post: A Profile of News Use on Social Networking Sites," *Computers in Human Behavior*, Vol. 28, No. 1, 2012, pp. 113–119.

Grinberg, Nir, Kenneth Joseph, Lisa Friedland, Briony-Swire-Thompson, and David Lazer, "Fake News on Twitter During the 2016 U.S. Presidential Election," *Science*, Vol. 363, No. 6425, 2019, pp. 374–378.

Gunther, Albert C., "Biased Press or Biased Public?" *Public Opinion Quarterly*, Vol. 56, No. 2, 1992, pp. 147–167.

Haller, Max, Markus Hadler, and Gerd Kaup, "Leisure Time in Modern Societies: A New Source of Boredom and Stress?" *Social Indicators Research*, Vol. 111, No. 2, 2013, pp. 403–434.

Hart, William, Dolores Albarracín, Alice H. Eagly, Inge Brechan, Matthew J. Lindberg, and Lisa Merrill, "Feeling Validated Versus Being Correct: A Meta-Analysis of Selective Exposure to Information," *Psychological Bulletin*, Vol. 135, No. 4, 2009, pp. 555–588.

Hastall, Matthias R., "Information Utility as Determinant of Media Choices," in Tilo Hartmann, ed., *Media Choice: A Theoretical and Empirical Overview*, New York: Routledge, 2009, pp. 149–166.

Hawkins, Robert P., Suzanne Pingree, Jacqueline Hitchon, Bradley W. Gorham, Prathna Kannaovakun, Eileen Gilligan, Barry Radler, Gudbjorg H. Kolbeins, and Toni Schmidt, "Predicting Selection and Activity in Television Genre Viewing," *Media Psychology*, Vol. 3, No. 3, 2001, pp. 237–264.

Hmielowski, Jay D., R. Lance Holbert, and Jayeon Lee, "Predicting the Consumption of Political TV Satire: Affinity for Political Humor, *The Daily Show*, and *The Colbert Report*," *Communication Monographs*, Vol. 78, No. 1, 2011, pp. 96–114.

Huang, Edgar, "The Causes of Youths' Low News Consumption and Strategies for Making Youths Happy News Consumers," *Convergence: The International Journal of Research into New Media Technologies*, Vol. 15, No. 1, 2009, pp. 105–122.

Iyengar, Shanto, and Kyu S. Hahn, "Red Media, Blue Media: Evidence of Ideological Selectivity in Media Use," *Journal of Communication*, Vol. 5, 2009, pp. 19–39.

Jakob, Nikolaus G., "No Alternatives? The Relationship Between Perceived Media Dependency, Use of Alternative Information Sources, and General Trust in Mass Media," *International Journal of Communication*, Vol. 4, 2010, pp. 589–606.

Johnson, Thomas J., and Barbara K. Kaye, "Cruising Is Believing? Comparing Internet and Traditional Sources on Media Credibility Measures," *Journalism and Mass Communication Quarterly*, Vol. 75, No. 2, 1998, pp. 325–340.

Jones, David A., "Why Americans Don't Trust the Media: A Preliminary Analysis," *Harvard International Journal of Press/Politics*, Vol. 9, No. 2, 2004, pp. 60–75.

Kaiser, Henry F., "The Application of Electronic Computers for Factor Analysis," *Educational and Psychological Measurement*, Vol. 20, No. 1, 1960, pp. 141–151.

Kavanagh, Jennifer, and Michael D. Rich, *Truth Decay: An Initial Exploration of the Diminishing Role of Facts and Analysis in American Public Life*, RR-2314-RC, 2018. As of September 3, 2019:
https://www.rand.org/pubs/research_reports/RR2314.html

Kayany, Joseph M., and Paul Yelsma, "Displacement Effects of Online Media in the Socio-Technical Contexts of Households," *Journal of Broadcasting & Electronic Media*, Vol. 44, No. 2, 2000, pp. 215–229.

Kaye, Barbara K., and Thomas J. Johnson, "From Here to Obscurity? Media Substitution Theory and Traditional Media in an Online World," *Journal of the American Society for Information Science and Technology*, Vol. 54, No. 3, 2003, pp. 260–273.

Kiousis, Spiro, "Public Trust of Mistrust? Perceptions of Media Credibility in the Information Age," *Mass Communication & Society*, Vol. 4, No. 4, 2001, pp. 381–403.

Knight Foundation, *An Online Experimental Platform to Assess Trust in the Media*, Miami, Fla., July 18, 2018. As of August 4, 2018:
https://knightfoundation.org/reports/
an-online-experimental-platform-to-assess-trust-in-the-media

Knight Foundation and Trust, Media and Democracy, "10 Reasons Why American Trust in the Media Is at an All-Time Low," *Medium*, January 15, 2018. As of August 4, 2018:
https://medium.com/trust-media-and-democracy/10-reasons-why-americans-dont-trust-the-media-d0630c125b9e

Kohring, Matthias, and Jörg Matthes, "Trust in News Media: Development and Validation of a Multidimensional Scale," *Communication Research*, Vol. 34, No. 2, 2007, pp. 231–252.

Krcmar, Marina, and Yuliya Strizhakova, "Uses and Gratifications as Media Choice," in Tilo Hartmann, ed., *Media Choice: A Theoretical and Empirical Overview*, New York: Routledge, 2009, pp. 53–69.

Lavrakas, Paul, "Response Bias," *Encyclopedia of Survey Research Methods*, Thousand Oaks, Calif.: Sage, 2008.

Lee, Angela M., "News Audiences Revisited: Theorizing the Link Between Audience Motivations and News Consumption," *Journal of Broadcasting & Electronic Media*, Vol. 57, No. 3, 2013, pp. 300–317.

Lee, Tien-Tsun, "Why They Don't Trust the Media: An Examination of Factors Predicting Trust," *American Behavioral Scientist*, Vol. 54, No. 1, 2010, pp. 8–21.

Leighley, Jan E., and Jonathan Nagler, *Who Votes Now? Demographics, Issues, Inequality, and Turnout in the United States*, Princeton, N.J.: Princeton University Press, 2013.

Liebler, Carolyn A., and Gary D. Sandefur, "Gender Differences in the Exchange of Social Support with Friends, Neighbors, and Co-Workers at Midlife," *Social Science Research*, Vol. 31, No. 3, 2002, pp. 364–391.

Liebowitz, Stan J., and Alejandro Zentner, "Clash of the Titans: Does Internet Use Reduce Television Viewing?" *Review of Economics and Statistics*, Vol. 94, No. 1, 2012, pp. 234–245.

Lin, Carolyn, "Modeling the Gratification-Seeking Process of Television Viewing," *Human Communication Research*, Vol. 20, No. 2, 1993, pp. 224–244.

Lin, Carolyn, Michael B. Salwen, Bruce Garrison, and Paul D. Driscoll, "Online News as a Functional Substitute for Offline News," in Michael B. Salwen, Bruce Garrison, and Paul D. Driscoll, eds., *Online News and the Public*, Mahwah, N.J.: Lawrence Erlbaum, 2005, pp. 237–256.

Mackay, Jenn Burleson, and Wilson Lowrey, "The Credibility Divide: Reader Trust of Online Newspapers and Blogs," *Journal of Media Sociology*, Vol. 3, Nos. 1–4, 2011, pp. 39–57.

Martin, Vivian B., "Attending the News: A Grounded Theory About a Daily Regimen," *Journalism*, Vol. 9, No. 1, 2008, pp. 76–94.

Mason, Liliana, *Uncivil Agreement: How Politics Became Our Identity*, Chicago, Ill.: University of Chicago Press, 2018.

Matsa, Katerina Eva, and Elisa Shearer, "News Use Across Social Media Platforms 2018," webpage, Pew Research Center, September 10, 2018. As of November 4, 2018:
http://www.journalism.org/2018/09/10/
news-use-across-social-media-platforms-2018/

McDonald, Steve, and Christine A. Mair, "Social Capital Across the Life Course: Age and Gendered Patterns of Network Resources," *Sociological Forum*, Vol. 25, No. 2, June 2010.

Merriam-Webster, "Filter Bubble," webpage, undated. As of August 4, 2018: https://www.merriam-webster.com/dictionary/filter%20bubbles

Meyer, Philip, "Defining and Measuring Credibility of Newspapers: Developing an Index," *Journalism Quarterly*, Vol. 65, No. 3, 1988, pp. 567–588.

Mitchell, Amy, Jeffrey Gottfried, Elisa Shearer, and Kristine Lu, *How Americans Encounter, Recall and Act Upon Digital News*, Washington, D.C.: Pew Research Center, February 9, 2017. As of August 4, 2018: http://www.journalism.org/2017/02/09/how-americans-encounter-recall-and-act-upon-digital-news/

Mitchell, Amy, Katie Simmons, Katerina Eva Matsa, and Laura Silver, "Publics Globally Want Unbiased News Coverage, but Are Divided on Whether Their News Media Deliver," Pew Research Center, January 11, 2018. As of August 4, 2018: http://www.pewglobal.org/2018/01/11/publics-globally-want-unbiased-news-coverage-but-are-divided-on-whether-their-news-media-deliver/

Mitchelstein, Eugenia, and Pablo J. Boczkowski, "Online News Consumption Research: An Assessment of Past Work and an Agenda for the Future," *New Media & Society*, Vol. 12, No. 7, 2010, pp. 1085–1102.

Newhagen, John, and Clifford Nass, "Differential Criteria for Evaluating Credibility of Newspapers and TV News," *Journalism Quarterly*, Vol. 66, No. 2, 1989, pp. 277–284.

Owen, Laura Hazard, "Here's Who Gets News from TV: The Elderly, Pew Finds (Again)," Neiman Lab, January 8, 2018. As of August 4, 2018: http://www.niemanlab.org/2018/01/heres-who-gets-news-from-tv-the-elderly-pew-finds-again/

Papacharissi, Zizi, and Alan M. Rubin, "Predictors of Internet Use," *Journal of Broadcasting & Electronic Media*, Vol. 44, No. 2, 2000, pp. 175–196.

Peters, Chris, "Journalism to Go," *Journalism Studies*, Vol. 13, Nos. 5–6, 2012, pp. 695–705.

Peters, Chris, and Marcel Jeroen Broersma, eds., *Rethinking Journalism: Trust and Participation in a Transformed News Landscape*, New York: Routledge, 2013.

Pew Research Center, *One-in-Ten Voters Online for Campaign '96*, Washington, D.C., December 16, 1996. As of August 4, 2018: http://assets.pewresearch.org/wp-content/uploads/sites/5/legacy-pdf/117.pdf

Pollard, Michael, and Matthew D. Baird, *The RAND American Life Panel: Technical Description*, Santa Monica, Calif.: RAND Corporation, RR-1651, 2017. As of September 3, 2019:
https://www.rand.org/pubs/research_reports/RR1651.html

Pollard, Michael, and Joshua Mendelsohn, "RAND Kicks Off 2016 Presidential Election Panel Survey," *The RAND Blog*, January 27, 2016. As of August 4, 2018:
https://www.rand.org/blog/2016/01/rand-kicks-off-2016-presidential-election-panel-survey.html

———, *Methodology of the 2016 Rand Presidential Election Panel Survey (PEPS)*, Santa Monica, Calif.: RAND Corporation, RR-1460-RC/UCLA, 2016. As of September 3, 2019:
https://www.rand.org/pubs/research_reports/RR1460.html

Price, Rande, "Oxford Research Documents the Alarming Rise of Disinformation on Social Media," *Digital Content Next*, September 21, 2018.

Prior, Markus, "News vs. Entertainment: How Increasing Media Choice Widens Gaps in Political Knowledge and Turnout," *American Journal of Political Science*, Vol. 49, No. 3, July 2005, pp. 577–592.

RAND Corporation, "Welcome to the ALP Data Pages," webpage, undated. As of September 5, 2019:
https://alpdata.rand.org

Rimmer, Tony, and David Weaver, "Different Questions, Different Answers? Media Use and Media Credibility," *Journalism Quarterly*, Vol. 64, No. 1, 1987, pp. 28–44.

Rubin, Alan M., "Uses and Gratifications: An Evolving Perspective of Media Effects," in Robin L. Nabi and Mary Beth Oliver, eds., *The SAGE Handbook of Media Processes and Effects*, Thousand Oaks, Calif.: SAGE Publications, 2009, pp. 147–159.

Ruggiero, Thomas E., "Uses and Gratifications Theory in the 21st Century," *Mass Communication & Society*, Vol. 3, No. 1, 2001, pp. 3–37.

Sarkisian, Natalia, and Naomi Gerstel, "Till Marriage Do Us Part: Adult Children's Relationships with Their Parents," *Journal of Marriage and Family*, Vol. 70, No. 2, 2008, pp. 360–376.

Schmidt, Christine, "Planted Stories? Fake News as Editorial Decisions? Trump or CNN? A Poll Examines the Public's Trust of Mainstream Media," Neiman Lab, April 3, 2018. As of August 4, 2018:
http://www.niemanlab.org/2018/04/planted-stories-fake-news-as-editorial-decisions-trump-or-cnn-a-poll-examines-the-publics-trust-of-mainstream-media/

Shearer, Elisa, "Audio and Podcasting Fact Sheet," webpage, Pew Research Center, July 12, 2018. As of August 4, 2018:
http://www.journalism.org/fact-sheet/audio-and-podcasting/

Shearer, Elisa, and Jeffrey Gottfried, "News Use Across Social Media Platforms 2017," webpage, Pew Research Center, September 7, 2017. As of August 4, 2018: http://www.journalism.org/2017/09/07/ news-use-across-social-media-platforms-2017/

Shoemaker, Pamela J., "Hardwired for News: Using Biological and Cultural Evolution to Explain Surveillance Function," *Journal of Communication*, Vol. 46, No. 3, 1996, pp. 32–47.

Stempel, Guido H., and Thomas Hargrove, "Mass Media Audiences in a Changing Media Environment," *Journalism & Mass Communication Quarterly*, Vol. 73, No. 3, September 1996, pp. 549–558.

Stroud, Natalie J., *Niche News: The Politics of News Choice*, New York: Oxford University Press, 2011.

Stroud, Natalie Jomini, and Jae Kook Lee, "Perceptions of Cable News Credibility," *Mass Communication and Society*, Vol. 16, No. 1, 2013, pp. 67–88.

Taneja, Harsh, James G. Webster, Edward C. Malthouse, and Thomas B. Ksiazek, "Media Consumption Across Platforms: Identifying User-Defined Repertoires," *New Media and Society*, Vol. 14, No. 6, 2012, pp. 951–968.

Tsfati, Yariv, and Joseph N. Cappella, "Do People Watch What They Do Not Trust? Exploring the Association Between News Media Skepticism and Exposure," *Communication Research*, Vol. 30, No. 5, 2003, pp. 504–529.

Twenge, Jean M., Gabrielle N. Martin, and Brian H. Spitzberg, "Trends in US Adolescents' Media Use, 1976–2016: The Rise of Digital Media, the Decline of TV, and the (Near) Demise of Print," *Psychology of Popular Media Culture*, August 2018.

U.S. Census, "Language Spoken at Home by Ability to Speak English for the Population 5 Years and over," webpage, 2017. As of August 4, 2018: https://factfinder.census.gov/bkmk/table/1.0/en/ACS/17_1YR/B16001

Van Damme, Kristin, Cédric Courtois, Karel Verbrugge, and Lieven De Marez, "What's APPening to News? A Mixed-Method Audience-Centred Study on Mobile News Consumption," *Mobile Media & Communication*, Vol. 3, No. 2, 2015, pp. 196–213.

Wanta, Wayne, and Yu-Wei Hu, "The Effects of Credibility, Reliance, and Exposure on Media Agenda-Setting: A Path Analysis Model," *Journalism Quarterly*, Vol. 71, No. 1, 1994, pp. 90–98.

Weldon, Michele, *Everyman News: The Changing American Front Page*, Columbia, Mo.: University of Missouri Press, 2008.

West, Mark Douglas, "Validating a Scale for the Measurement of Credibility: A Covariance Structure Modeling Approach," *Journalism Quarterly*, Vol. 71, No. 1, 1994, pp. 159–168.

Westley, Bruce H., and Werner J. Severin, "Some Correlates of Media Credibility," *Journalism Quarterly* , Vol. 41, No. 3, 1964, pp. 325–335.

Westlund, Oscar, and Mathias A. Färdigh, "Accessing the News in an Age of Mobile Media: Tracing Displacing and Complementary Effects of Mobile News on Newspapers and Online News," *Mobile Media & Communication*, Vol. 3, No. 1, 2015, pp. 53–74.

Wheeless, Lawrence R., "The Effects of Attitude, Credibility, and Homophily on Selective Exposure to Information," *Speech Monographs*, Vol. 41, 1974, pp. 329–338.

Wolf, Cornelia, and Anna Schnauber, "News Consumption in the Mobile Era," *Digital Journalism*, Vol. 3, No. 5, 2015, pp. 759–776.